BROOKLYN'S
PLYMOUTH CHURCH
IN THE CIVIL WAR ERA

A MINISTRY OF FREEDOM

FRANK DECKER,
ASSISTED BY LOIS ROSEBROOKS

Charleston

THE
History
PRESS

D1069319

Published by The History Press
Charleston, SC 29403
www.historypress.net

Cover images: Front: Top image from the Collection of Plymouth Church; bottom image from the author's collection. Back: Top left and right images from the Collection of Plymouth Church, and center image from the Brady-Handy Photograph Collection, Library of Congress; bottom image from the Collection of Plymouth Church.

First published 2013

Manufactured in the United States

ISBN 978.1.60949.810.8

Library of Congress CIP data applied for.

CONTENTS

Acknowledgements

For anyone doing research about Plymouth Church or its membership, its church records are an invaluable resource. A number of church documents were donated to the Brooklyn Historical Society and have been carefully indexed and archived. The church continues to maintain more documents than were given to the historical society. Lois Rosebrooks, as director of the church's History Ministry Services, has supervised the archiving of documents, the collection of pictures and memorabilia and the organization of research materials relating to Plymouth Church history. Through her tours of the church, she has told the Underground Railroad narrative of the church to thousands of schoolchildren and visitors. At the historical society, Director Deborah Schwartz and Julie May, the librarian for images, were most helpful.

The librarians at several locations assisted the research for this book: the Forty-second Street branch of the New York Public Library for the study of the microfilm of the Lewis Tappan Papers; the Schomburg Center for Research in Black Culture, a research unit of the New York Public Library, for the study of the microfilm of the papers of the American Missionary Association; the Library of the New-York Historical Society; the Beinecke Rare Book and Manuscript Library of the Yale University Library and Manuscripts and Archives of Sterling Memorial Library at Yale for the Beecher family papers; and the Congregational Library in Boston.

Edith Bartley, a member of Plymouth Church who has a deep understanding of the history of the church, was most helpful in reading the manuscript and giving her comments.

Many people helped by suggesting approaches we should take. We are grateful for the advice of Christopher Moore, curator and research historian at the Schomburg Center for Research in Black Culture; Tim Driscoll and Richard Hourahan of the Queens County Historical Society; Sheri Jackson and Diane Miller of the National Underground Railroad Network to Freedom of the National Park Service; Don Papson, president of the North Country Underground Railroad Historical Association; Cordell Reeves of the New York State Office of Parks, Recreation and Historic Preservation; Margaret Bendroff, executive director of the Congregational Library; Jeff Richardson, historian, and Anthony Cucchiara, archivist, of Green-Wood Cemetery; and Mary Kay Ricks, author of *Escape on the Pearl*.

It has been a pleasure working with The History Press commissioning editor Whitney Landis, whose insightful edits, comments and suggestions have improved the text and choice of images.

I owe a debt of gratitude to friends, too many to name, who encouraged me in this project. My family also helped in many ways. My wife, Marianne, read and commented on text and took photographs to be used as images in the book. Our daughter, Anne, prepared the map of the Underground Railroad. And our sons, Keil and Alec, read the text and made helpful comments and suggestions.

INTRODUCTION

Henry Ward Beecher—minister of Brooklyn's famous Plymouth Church—has been called "the most famous man in America." His story has been told many times: he had a flair for the dramatic that included conducting sensational mock slave auctions and delivering sermons and speeches that newspapers across America often quoted. He wrote articles that he signed with an asterisk and, therefore, was called the first "star" reporter. Abraham Lincoln invited him to deliver the address at the raising of the flag at Fort Sumter at the end of the Civil War because of his support of the Union cause during the war.

By contrast, while Beecher was certainly important, Plymouth Church was much more than Beecher. Fascinating people formed the Plymouth community in the years from 1847 to 1870. Beecher's sister, novelist Harriet Beecher Stowe, did not live in Brooklyn, but she was a church member and visited often to be with her brother. She was the best-known author of the nineteenth century. When Lincoln met her at the White House during the Civil War, the president is reported to have greeted her with, "Is this the little lady who made this great war?" Plymouth member Lewis Tappan had been a leader of the effort to raise money for the defense of the Africans captured on the *Amistad*. He was a founder of antislavery societies and was active in helping fugitives escape from slavery on the Underground Railroad. Another member, George Whipple, was one of the "rebels" who left Lane Theological Seminary to go to school at Oberlin and who later came to New York and Brooklyn to work with Tappan at the American Missionary

Association. Henry C. Bowen, Tappan's son-in-law, was owner and became publisher of the *Independent* newspaper. Working at the paper was Joshua Leavitt, who joined the Church of the Pilgrims but became a member of the Plymouth Church community—when he died, his funeral was held at Plymouth Church, and he was eulogized by Beecher as a close friend. Plymouth member Theodore Tilton became editor in chief of the paper in the 1860s.

Other members of the Plymouth congregation contributed money to support the activities of the church, volunteered hours of work for its ministries and eventually fought in the war.

In addition, the Plymouth Church community included other black and white abolitionists. African Americans Reverend Charles B. Ray and Reverend Amos N. Freeman were close friends of Plymouth Church, as were Reverend James W.C. Pennington and Frederick Douglass. It seemed that church members knew people all over the United States, enough that Brooklyn was tied to upstate New York, Cincinnati and Oberlin in Ohio and New England. They also reached out to antislavery activists in the United Kingdom and Canada.

We uncovered this story of compelling people because, as longtime members of Congregational churches, we knew that a Congregational church, by definition, is not just about the minister; it is also about the congregation. Our experience as members of the governing body of Plymouth Church told us that the church was more than just Beecher. We believed that Henry Ward Beecher and his congregation worked together as a team.[1]

To support our hypothesis, we used church records to identify members of the congregation in the Civil War era and then sought more information about them from U.S. Census data, Brooklyn City Directories and antislavery society membership lists. We also consulted newspapers including the *Independent*, the *Brooklyn Eagle* and the *New York Times*. In the process, we found that Plymouth Church had a remarkable group of people that worked together with Beecher.

Members and friends of the church were driven by religious principles to abolish slavery and support enslaved people when they were emancipated. When Plymouth Church was gathered in 1847, Brooklyn was becoming a city inhabited by waves of New Englanders moving there to get jobs in New York City—the mercantile and financial center of the United States. When they came to Brooklyn, they established the Congregational churches they had known in New England.

Members of these churches sought to practice their faith "purely," as the New Testament described early Christian churches in the Acts of the Apostles and the letters of Paul. They believed in the Creation story in Genesis—that people were created by God in his image—and they understood that the Declaration of Independence incorporated this idea in the statement that America's founders held "these truths to be self-evident, that all men are created equal, that they are endowed by their Creator with certain unalienable Rights, that among these are Life, Liberty and the pursuit of Happiness." Such a foundational statement in the Bible and America's founding document was inconsistent with people being held in bondage. Also contradicting the institution of slavery were the gospel commandments to love one's neighbor as one's self and the "golden rule" to do unto others as you would have them do unto you.[2]

In its ministry of freedom, Plymouth Church set the seemingly impossible goal of helping America right the wrong of American slavery. It would take persuasion. It would take time and patience. It would take determination. This is their story.

THE EDMONSON SISTERS

Paul Edmonson came to the antislavery society in New York City seeking help to save his two teenaged daughters, fifteen-year-old Mary and thirteen-year-old Emily, from a future enslaved as prostitutes in New Orleans. He was a free black person, but his wife was enslaved, and therefore, their daughters were, too. The only hope he had to save his daughters was to raise enough money to purchase their freedom. That hope was slim, as the challenges were high. But he knew no other way.

Some four and a half months earlier, on April 15, 1848, Edmonson's daughters had joined seventy-five others on board the schooner *Pearl* in a bold attempt to escape from slavery in the District of Columbia. Ironically, the escape took place when free people in Washington were celebrating apparent victories of democratic forces in the European Revolutions of 1848. They got away, but when the wind died down, a pursuing steamboat captured them. After the ship and its passengers had been towed back to the capital city, Mary and Emily were sold to a slave trader, Joseph Bruin. He intended to take them to New Orleans and sell them as "fancy girls"—that is, girls for whom men take a fancy. By this means, he thought he could get the best price. He said that he believed he could sell them for $2,250.

In May, Bruin sent the girls by ship to New Orleans. They arrived there in mid-June but did not remain long. Three thousand had died from yellow fever in the previous year, and Bruin feared that an epidemic might occur again, threatening his investment. Furthermore, the slave trader returned them, he later wrote, "upon the positive assurance that the money for them would

be raised if they were brought back."[3] The girls were brought back to Washington in July.

Before the girls were taken to New Orleans, Paul Edmonson had not been able to raise money to purchase their freedom. Now that they had come back, he had another chance. A huge problem was that $2,250 was a small fortune (in 2012 dollars, it would be $67,250). Edmonson owned a forty-acre farm outside Washington, but selling that or taking out a loan (using it as collateral) would not raise enough to save his daughters.

Thus, Edmonson needed help. William L. Chaplin, a leader of the Underground Railroad in Washington, tried to help, but he was not successful. As September approached, they decided to go to New York, where Chaplin was a member of the antislavery organization. They hoped that his friends might raise the funds.

GEN WM L, CHAPLIN.

Lith.B.W.Thayer&C?

Top: The Edmonson sisters were photographed in New York City in 1852, when Mary was nineteen years old and Emily was seventeen. At that time, they and their mother, Amelia, met with Harriet Beecher Stowe. Stowe described her interview of Amelia and the girls' story in her book *A Key to Uncle Tom's Cabin*. *Historical Society of Washington, D.C.*

Bottom: William L. Chaplin. *Library of Congress.*

In preparation for the trip, Edmonson and Chaplin collected statements from various people attesting to the excellent character of the girls. Chaplin also talked with slave trader Bruin, who agreed that he would not take the girls to be sold for a period of twenty-five days, so long as Edmonson paid $1,200 within fifteen days. That was a tight schedule, but it was the best he could negotiate.

ANTISLAVERY SOCIETY GOES TO WORK

Edmonson took the train to Jersey City and the ferry to New York City, where he went to the offices of the American and Foreign Anti-Slavery Society, New York's antislavery office. The corresponding secretary of the society was sixty-year-old Lewis Tappan, a man with many contacts among New York businessmen. He had been a successful merchant as well as founder of the mercantile credit agency that later became Dun & Bradstreet. For fifteen years, he had been one of the leaders of the antislavery movement in New York City and the country. In 1833, he had been a founder of the New York City Anti-Slavery Society and the American Anti-Slavery Society. He had directly contributed money to the antislavery cause and had also raised money. He was the treasurer of an antislavery missionary organization, the American Missionary Association, of which he had been a founder. From 1839 to 1841, he and two friends composed the committee to raise funds for the defense of the *Amistad* Africans. Leaders of the antislavery society and the missionary association included black and white ministers who could reach out to churches and communities in the New York area. Chaplin had directed Edmonson to the man and organization most able to raise funds to free his daughters, if that could be done.

Even though many abolitionists opposed compensating slave owners for freeing enslaved people, those at the antislavery office immediately began to circulate an appeal to well-to-do New Yorkers. Those who were contacted, however, were reluctant to give money because the amount asked for two teenaged girls was, they said, too large an amount to be believable.

Thus, those at the antislavery office asked a lawyer in Washington to try to negotiate with the slave trader for a lower price. He told the New Yorkers that the price was high because of the purpose for which the girls would be sold. "The truth is, *and is confessed to be*," he said, "*their destination is prostitution;*

Lewis Tappan. *Collection of Plymouth Church.*

of this you would be satisfied on seeing them; they are of elegant form, and fine faces."[4]

Almost two weeks later, William Chaplin wrote to say that Bruin would not lower the price he had demanded. Chaplin suggested that, if they had not already done so, they might try to raise money through churches.

The printer William Harned, a member of the antislavery society, sent Edmonson to his friend, Reverend James W.C. Pennington, minister of the Shiloh Presbyterian Church, the first African American Presbyterian church in Manhattan. Pennington grew up enslaved in Maryland. Trained as a blacksmith, he ran away. He had hoped to study at Yale Theological Seminary but was turned down. The school did, however, let him study in the library. After studying there, he was ordained. As minister of a Congregational church in Hartford, Connecticut, he proved to be a good pastor and an effective organizer. He came to know Lewis Tappan and worked with his *Amistad* committee. With Tappan, he formed a missionary society for African Americans to support African missions. This society was a foundation of the American Missionary Association. In 1849, he wrote an autobiographical slave narrative, *The Fugitive Blacksmith*.[5]

Pennington said that Edmonson appeared at his study, "an aged coloured man of tall and slender form. I saw depicted on his countenance anxiety bordering on despair." On the next Sunday, as he said, Pennington "threw the case before my people." The congregation of the Shiloh Church did not have many wealthy members, and the members may have had family members of their own that they wanted to help escape slavery. Church members were sympathetic and helped as much as they could, but they were only able to raise fifty dollars.[6]

Reverend James W.C. Pennington.
Author's collection.

On September 30, Bruin's deadline for payment came due. Twenty-five days had passed since his letter of September 5. Bruin kept up the pressure on Paul Edmonson and those who were helping him. As time went by without receiving any money, Bruin organized a coffle of his enslaved persons chained together in a line to be walked overland to Alabama or Mississippi. Initially, he planned to include Mary and Emily in the coffle, but at the last minute, he withdrew them.

PLANNING A FUNDRAISING RALLY

As the next step, a committee of the Methodist Episcopal Church was organized to coordinate fundraising. The antislavery office chose that church because the Edmonson sisters worshiped at a church of that denomination in Washington and had attended Methodist classes there.

Meeting on October 14, they scheduled a fundraising rally to take place on October 23, 1848, at the Broadway Tabernacle, a Congregational church meetinghouse in New York City that was often used for large meetings. In addition to Methodist clergy, they invited ministers of other denominations to participate. To encourage fundraising, they published a pamphlet describing the Edmonsons' plight, including the statements and correspondence about the girls that had been collected by William Chaplin and the antislavery society.

On the day of the rally, Edmonson was advised to go across the East River from New York City to find Reverend Henry Ward Beecher in Brooklyn and tell him his story. The persons most likely to have given this advice were Lewis Tappan or William Harned, as both lived in Brooklyn and knew Beecher. Tappan's daughter and son-in-law were among the founders of Beecher's Plymouth Church in Brooklyn. In fact, his son-in-law, Henry Bowen, had vigorously pursued Beecher to accept the call as Plymouth's minister. Harned was a part of the Plymouth Church community. Furthermore, they might have suggested that Edmonson approach Beecher because they had seen the *Brooklyn Daily Eagle* article of four months earlier reporting that Beecher had given a "deeply moving address" at a meeting for the purpose of raising money to free from slavery the son of a black man who was a member of a local Baptist church.[7]

To travel from Manhattan to Brooklyn, Edmonson took a short, five-minute ride from Fulton Street in Manhattan only seven hundred yards across the East River to Fulton Street in Brooklyn. High over the terminal was Brooklyn Heights, a bluff rising to eighty-five feet above the river near Fulton Street on the north end and sloping down both to the east and the south. Leaving the ferry, Edmonson walked up Fulton Street for two-tenths of a mile and then up Henry Street for another one-tenth of a mile to the corner of Cranberry Street. That was the center of the city of Brooklyn,

Opposite, top: This print shows the Brooklyn Fulton Ferry Terminal, where Paul Edmonson arrived in Brooklyn to meet with Reverend Henry Ward Beecher. *Author's collection.*

Opposite, bottom: This 1855 map shows downtown Brooklyn looking west toward New York City. The Fulton Ferry Terminal is located to the left of the point under the letter *a* in "East River." From the terminal, the route of Fulton Street is inland until it turns to the right, marking the base of Brooklyn Heights. Furman Street next to the river is at waterside, and Columbia Street shown on the map next to it is on the Heights. The location of Plymouth Church is shown as a line from Orange and Cranberry Streets between Hicks and Henry Streets. *Collection of Plymouth Church.*

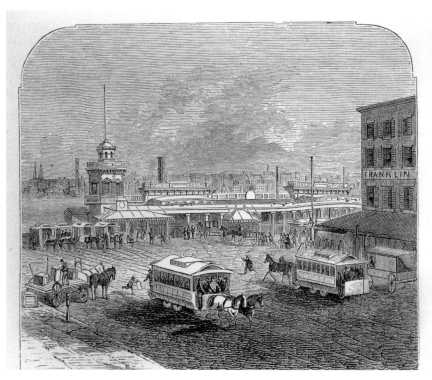

as it had been when Brooklyn was a village, fourteen years earlier. City hall was under construction. Half a block west from the corner of Cranberry Street was Plymouth Church. Houses were being built on the Heights, but many lots were vacant, and fields from its previous farms were still present. Beecher's house was next door to Plymouth Church. As was later described, Edmonson "ascended the steps to ring the door-bell, but his heart failed him—he sat down on the steps weeping!"[8]

Beecher found Edmonson there, brought him inside the house and heard his story. Would Beecher go to the rally at the Broadway Tabernacle that night and plead for his children? Indeed, Beecher agreed to do so.

Henry Ward Beecher at the Broadway Tabernacle

Where the rally took place influenced what happened that night. The Broadway Tabernacle resembled an amphitheater in a square one hundred feet on a side. The curved ceiling with a shallow dome made the acoustics excellent. Speakers could be heard easily throughout the room that seated 2,500 people. A large stage projected into the room where the audience was seated. The pews curved around the stage. As would happen in outdoor revivals, people surrounded the speaker, who had to move around the stage to engage everyone in the room. It was a church that had been built especially for, and according to the design specifications of, the revivalist Reverend Charles Grandison Finney. He had based the interior design on his experience at the Chatham Street Chapel, a theater in the round that had been used for circuses until Lewis Tappan had arranged to convert it into a church. Finney used it from 1832 to 1836. Importantly, people sitting in the audience could see others around the room. Some people that night might have been persuaded to give money when they saw others giving.

Beecher was not the only person to speak at the Broadway Tabernacle that night. But he was the one people remembered. At thirty-five years old, he was younger than some of the other ministers who spoke. Beecher did not look like a New York minister. Even though he had grown up in the East, he had spent thirteen years in the West. Having gone to seminary in Cincinnati, he had pastored churches at Lawrenceburg and Indianapolis, Indiana. He looked like a westerner, someone from the frontier. His hair was longer than was fashionable

Above: Interior of the Broadway Tabernacle.
Park Slope Gallery.

Left: This photograph of Reverend Henry
Ward Beecher was taken circa 1850–55. *Brady-
Handy Photograph Collection, Library of Congress.*

for New York. His dress was careless, and he wore western boots. Plymouth Church member Susan Howard described him as "rather rough and 'dreadful homely.'" But he was animated. She said that he "can turn from grave to gay or *vice versa* about as quick as any fellow I ever saw." She continued, "There is a sort of fascination about the man which I should think was produced in a great measure by his earnestness, his fervor, his impulsiveness, his seeming naturalness. He carries one along with him by the power of his own flow, like some mighty river taking the very rocks upon his bosom of impetuosity."[9]

From the start of his talk, Beecher made it clear that he was not talking about slavery or antislavery in general. This evening was about people in trouble, specifically about Mary and Emily Edmonson, two young girls in a Washington, D.C., slave pen. And it was about their father, Paul Edmonson. What was being discussed that evening was, he said, "a plain question of humanity, and will admit of but one answer."

He also admitted that the price being asked for the freedom of the two girls was outrageously high. He wished it were less. People were not being asked to buy the freedom of every slave on the market. This was a unique case. "I should be ashamed if it were written down, that such an assembly was gathered here of more than two thousand souls...and the poor pittance of $2,000 could not be raised."[10]

Beecher pointed out Paul Edmonson. He described him as a "distressed father." He urged the audience to put themselves in his position. He said, "His sons are long ago sold as slaves to labor on Southern plantations. His daughters, unless we can do something to detain them, must go too, to a worse fate. But I trust in God and I trust in you that it shall not be heard from New York that an appeal like this was not [*sic*] made in vain, and that you will make it heard that these girls, must not, shall not, be slaves—they shall be free."[11]

As he was speaking, pleading the Edmonsons' case, Beecher used the space to advantage. He engaged each person in the audience, walking back and forth on the stage. Leaning forward to reach out, Beecher used gestures to draw everyone in. His voice rose and fell according to his subject. Because of the acoustics, all could hear him clearly.

An eyewitness described what happened. Beecher dramatized a slave auction for the audience. The enslaved person was examined and described in terms of his physical attributes. As the observer recalled, "He made the scene as one of Hogarth's pictures and as lurid as a Rembrandt." Then he became an actor, playing the role of the slave auctioneer, using the cadences he had heard when he was in seminary at Cincinnati and visited across the Ohio River in the slave state of Kentucky, where he observed enslaved people being sold at auction.

"And more than all that, gentlemen, they say he is one of those praying Methodist niggers; who bids? A thousand—fifteen hundred—two thousand—twenty-five hundred! Going, going! Last call! *Gone!*"[12]

The impact on the audience was stunning, as was the result. The money needed to purchase the freedom of Paul Edmonson's teenage daughters, Mary and Emily, was raised.

THE SISTERS' VICTORY RALLY

Six and a half weeks later, on December 7, Beecher returned to the Broadway Tabernacle to introduce the Edmonson sisters at a victory rally. Many of those who had provided the funds for their freedom were undoubtedly there. Beecher thanked them for their generosity.

Beecher told the audience that his "friend," Joseph Bruin, had been offended by what he had said about him at the October 23 rally. Bruin had said that he was a "magnanimous, noble, most Christian slave trader." But Bruin had complained that Beecher and other abolitionists would not touch him with a "ten-foot-pole." Beecher's response that "I think we would" brought roars of laughter.[13]

Sculptures of the Edmonson sisters are at the base of the Henry Ward Beecher statue in Beecher Garden within the Plymouth Church complex. The sculptor, Gutzon Borglum, whose last work was Mount Rushmore, recognized the significance of the event. He depicted Mary reaching out with her right hand while comforting her younger sister, Emily. *Author's collection.*

The press carried the story of the freedom auction and of the celebration. One of the newspapers was a newly established paper, the *New York Independent*, which had been founded by a group of proprietors that included Henry Chandler Bowen, a founder of Plymouth Church and the son-in-law of Lewis Tappan. Tappan's longtime colleague in the antislavery wars, Joshua Leavitt, became the managing editor of the *Independent*. Although he had practiced law and been ordained as a Congregational minister, Leavitt became a writer, editor and publisher of abolitionist literature, serving as editor of the *Emancipator*, the *New York Evangelist* and other periodicals. He was also a spokesman for the Liberty Party, of which he was a founder. And he was one of three men—the others being Lewis Tappan and Simeon Jocelyn—who composed the committee to raise funds for the defense of the *Amistad* captives.[14]

As the result of the Edmonson sisters' freedom auction, several things happened. Beecher became well known as a dramatic speaker and personality throughout New York and Brooklyn. For the first time since coming to Plymouth Church, he worked with abolitionists who were actively supporting the freedom of individuals seeking to escape slavery. This introduction attracted like-minded people who participated in a growing congregation. Together, Beecher and the people of Plymouth Church developed into a community of members and black and white friends that became a center of antislavery activity.

CHAPTER 1

GATHERING PLYMOUTH CHURCH

John Tasker Howard, known to his friends as "Tasker," saw an opportunity he could not pass up. As a businessman, he was used to seizing opportunities. Now, in June 1846, he planned to establish a new Congregational church in Brooklyn.

While it was unheard of for laypersons of other denominations to found churches, Congregationalist laity had a long history from colonial times of doing so. Congregational churches are Trinitarian Christian churches, descended from Puritan churches of colonial New England. Governed by their congregations, they are "autonomous" and not governed by higher ecclesiastical authority.

This portrait of John Tasker Howard was in a frame with a metal plaque describing him as "the founder of Plymouth Church." *Collection of Plymouth Church.*

The Church of the Pilgrims was Brooklyn's first Congregational church. The church building was designed by Richard Upjohn, the English-born architect who had previously designed Trinity Church, Wall Street, in Manhattan. Called in 1846, Reverend Richard Salter Storrs, its first minister, served until 1900. He was one of the three original editors of the *Independent*. In 1934, the Church of the Pilgrims merged with Plymouth Church. *Author's collection.*

A year and a half before, in December 1844, Tasker had transferred his membership from the First Presbyterian Church of Brooklyn to become a founding member of the newly formed Church of the Pilgrims. Until recently, Congregational churches had not been established in Brooklyn and New York City.

Just days before Tasker decided, he attended a meeting held for the purpose of calling a minister for the Church of the Pilgrims. At the meeting, members had voted almost unanimously to call Reverend Richard Salter Storrs of Brookline, Massachusetts, to be their minister. Only one person had not voted for Reverend Storrs: Tasker.

Instead, Tasker voted to call Reverend Henry Ward Beecher, the young minister of the Second Presbyterian Church in Indianapolis, Indiana.[15] He had not met Beecher, but he had heard about him. Beecher's father was Reverend Lyman Beecher, one of the best-known preachers in the country, a man who played a prominent role in the Second Great Awakening, a revival that had taken the country by storm twenty years earlier. The question was: how could Tasker get Henry Ward Beecher to come to Brooklyn?

PERSUADING HENRY WARD BEECHER

To begin with, Tasker needed a vacant pulpit. He had an idea about how to accomplish that. Since he had previously been a member of the First Presbyterian Church and knew its members, he had learned that the Presbyterians would be vacating their church building and moving to a new one that was under construction. The building, called the "Brick Church," had been the first church built on Brooklyn Heights. When it was dedicated on April 24, 1823, the *Brooklyn Star* had described it as being in the Gothic style and "very neat and commodious."[16]

Thus, within days after he had cast his vote, Tasker met Cyrus P. Smith, the former mayor of Brooklyn and the president of the board of trustees of the First Presbyterian Church, on the ferry between Brooklyn and New York City. During that short ride, Tasker learned that the building was for sale and secured an option to purchase it. He bound the bargain by paying $2,000 of his own money. Then he approached friends to help him buy it. Tasker did not have trouble, as he was described as having "such a genial, sympathetic and affectionate nature that he made warm friends on every side." Having persuaded three friends to join him, Tasker and Cyrus Smith signed the contract of sale on June 11, 1846, to take effect when the Presbyterians moved.[17]

Throughout the fall and winter of 1846 and the spring of 1847, Tasker and his friends—David Hale of the Broadway Tabernacle and Henry Bowen and Seth Hunt, both of the Church of the Pilgrims—made plans for founding the church. The four also laid the groundwork for persuading Beecher to come to Brooklyn. From the start, they were in contact with William Cutter, a New York merchant living in Brooklyn, whose former partner was a member of Beecher's church. Cutter traveled and made a point of meeting with Beecher

Façade of Plymouth Church's original building on Cranberry Street, also called the "Brick Church," as it appeared on a snowy day in 1892 in a photograph by Julius Wilcox. At that time, the church building was being used as Plymouth Church's Sabbath School. The building to the left was where Beecher lived in 1848 when Paul Edmonson asked him to plead his case at the Broadway Tabernacle rally. *Brooklyn Public Library, Brooklyn Collection.*

Henry Chandler Bowen, oil painting by James Sawyer, circa 1886. *Historic New England.*

in Indianapolis, taking him on "fishing excursions, on drives and other amusements," as Beecher recalled years later. By March 1847, Henry Bowen, whose distant cousin was a member of Beecher's church, started to correspond with Beecher.[18]

To introduce Beecher to Brooklyn and allow those founding the church to meet and hear him, Cutter arranged with the American Home Missionary Society to invite Beecher to address the society's annual meeting in New York City during "Anniversary Week" in May 1847.[19] Since the Presbyterians were moving at that time, Tasker and his friends invited Beecher to preach at the first worship services at their new church.

As it turned out, Beecher was a hit. For the address at the missionary society, he appeared before an audience of well-dressed ministers looking like a country bumpkin in "rusty" and ill-fitting clothes. As he started to speak, he introduced himself by saying that he could tell his audience about peddlers distributing the devil's literature on western steamboats. The reason was, he said, "I can go among them as you, brethren, could not; for you see that nobody would ever suspect me of being a preacher." Looking at his rustic appearance, the New York audience started to laugh with him. As one biographer stated, "That opening sentence established his reputation, and he held his audiences spellbound from that time on."[20]

In the coming weeks, prayer meetings were held at which people were invited to join the church membership. Twenty-one people declared their intentions to become members. Documents for the formation of a church were prepared, approved by the new members and by a council of ministers and delegates from other churches. The members voted to call Henry Ward Beecher as their minister. Finally, they decided on "Plymouth Church" as the name for their new church.[21]

Even before the new members voted, Henry Bowen had written Beecher about a call. Bowen, tall and intense, was "a man of rare executive ability; prompt, quick to conceive" and acted quickly. He and Tasker Howard were worried that Beecher might accept a call from a Boston church before he knew he would receive one from Brooklyn. In due course, Beecher received a call to be the associate minister of Park Street Church in Boston, and the senior minister wrote him a letter urging him to come. By contrast, those at Plymouth wrote many letters. Not only did they write to Beecher, they also corresponded with his father, Lyman, and with Reverend Nathaniel Taylor at Yale, his father's close friend. To the frustration of those at Plymouth, Beecher took his time responding. Finally, he submitted his resignation to his Indianapolis church, declined the position at Park Street Church and accepted Plymouth's call on August 19, 1847.[22]

One of the reasons for his decision to come to Brooklyn, he said, was that he didn't "want to build on another's foundation, and I must confess that I find myself very strongly attracted to your enterprise, because here I could start my own church my own way, and build it from the ground as I think it ought to be."[23] What appealed to Beecher was that Plymouth Church was new and a place where he could establish a legacy.

The letter that Beecher sent to accept Plymouth's call was enclosed in an envelope sealed with a picture-seal, "in vogue in those days," showing a gate ajar and bearing the motto, "I'm all unhinged." When they received it, Tasker Howard and Henry Bowen became unhinged. Tasker recalled that "it would probably seem rather a comical sight to the younger members of the church to see Mr. Bowen and myself in each other's arms, crying and laughing and capering around like a couple of school-boys; yet that sight might have been seen the evening that Mr. Bowen came to my house with a letter which he had received from Mr. Beecher."[24]

BEECHER COMES TO BROOKLYN

Henry Ward Beecher arrived in Brooklyn and preached his first sermons on October 10, 1847. In these sermons, he defined the Plymouth Church ministry. At the morning worship service, he preached on "Jesus Christ as the source of true religion and the power of personal character." At evening worship, he preached on "the relation of the Church to the public ethical problems of the day—specifically, its duty to deal honestly and courageously with intemperance and with slavery." One church member said about the evening service, "to the astonishment of all, and dissatisfaction of some, he laid aside the doctrinal theologies of the morning, in favor of the living issues of the times, and boldly and clearly defined the position he had taken and intended to hold in reference to slavery, temperance, war, and general reform."[25]

These two sermons encompassed the gospel and the application of the gospel to moral issues of the day, including slavery, that had been a centerpiece of the evangelical reform movement growing out of the Second Great Awakening. As Beecher said at another time, "My earnest desire is that slavery may be destroyed by the manifest power of Christianity." Each year prior to the collection of the pew rents, he reasserted his opposition to slavery so that no one would be misled about his stand on the issue.[26]

Plymouth Church's antislavery ministry attracted abolitionists because few ministers and churches openly raised slavery as an issue. It was considered to be an issue too hot to touch. In recent years, the Presbyterian denomination had split over the issue.

By the end of 1847, the members of the congregation had grown from the original 21 to 56 men and women. A year later, at the end of 1848, Plymouth Church had 202 men and women as members. In addition, many people who were not members attended services and participated in other church activities.

One biographer wrote that "[t]he little church was overcrowded," as people came to hear Beecher. The increase in church membership can be attributed, at least in part, to Reverend Beecher's dramatic preaching. It also was likely the result of the growth of Brooklyn's population. In 1823, when the Brick Church was established, the village of Brooklyn had a population of less than ten thousand people. When Brooklyn was incorporated as a city in 1834, its population was sixteen thousand, and Kings County had fewer than twenty-five thousand residents. The 1845 New York State Census reported that the population of Brooklyn was just under sixty thousand, and the 1850 United States Census reported that it was almost ninety-seven thousand, an increase of more than 60 percent in five years.[27]

Another reason for the growth in membership seems to have come from Beecher's belief that "the first five years of the life of a church would determine the history of that church, and give to it its position and genius; that if the earliest years of a church were controversial or barren, it would take scores of years to right it; but if a church were consecrated and active and energetic during the first five years of its life, it would probably go on through generations developing the same features." To achieve this end, Beecher encouraged Plymouth Church to be "a singing people" because he believed that singing brought about community. Also, he had weekly meetings in addition to the Sunday services. These included a Tuesday evening "lecture" for adults, a Thursday evening "sociable" for fellowship and a prayer meeting on Friday evening.[28] In addition, Plymouth was reaching out, not only in its antislavery ministry but also in "planting" new churches, first in other parts of Brooklyn and later in other parts of the country.

A New Meetinghouse

On January 13, 1849, a little more than four weeks after Beecher had introduced the Edmonson sisters at the rally celebrating their freedom, a fire damaged the Brick Church. The damage to the building was estimated to be about $4,000, but according to the newspaper, this was covered by insurance with two companies.[29]

Members immediately assessed the damage and met to decide what to do. Even though they could have repaired the building, they searched for a rationale to construct a new worship space. One reported assertion was that "the accommodations were far from sufficient." Another was that the seats were "not convenient." Also, the building was "especially ill ventilated." Furthermore, without further explanation and contrary to the idea that the "little church was overcrowded," the meeting report noted, "There are multitudes who refuse to attend service in the church from reasons of health." At the end of the meeting, those present voted unanimously to construct a new church building.[30]

The next step was to come up with plans. After Henry Bowen examined how they would fund a new building, they decided that instead of selling the property they owned, they would tear down the structure on the Orange Street end of their property in back of the Brick Church to build a new meetinghouse there.

Beecher described his ideas for the new building to be constructed. He "insisted" on a building that would seat a congregation of 2,000. At the time of the fire, the membership was 202, and now Beecher was seeking a worship space to seat ten times that number. Some thought that to be "extravagant." In the end, the congregation took the risk and built a worship space with a seating capacity that it could grow into.

Interior of Plymouth Church was designed to seat 2,050, which was less than the 2,500 of the Broadway Tabernacle. By use of extra chairs or stools, Plymouth could seat 2,800, while the Tabernacle could seat 3,000. *Author's collection.*

In addition, Beecher had two ideas he wanted incorporated into the interior design. First, he wanted the new building to have the features of a New England meetinghouse, with a space that was symmetrical, light and simple in design. A growing number of New Englanders were moving to Brooklyn, and he wanted them to come to Plymouth Church and feel as if they were in familiar surroundings. Second, he wanted the "auditorium," as they called it, adapted to his style of preaching. The design he described included the features he had experienced at the Broadway Tabernacle.

The congregation acted quickly, as members must have wanted to maintain the momentum of a growing church. Three weeks after the fire had occurred, plans were presented and explained at length. When approved, construction was prepared. While this was happening, worship services were held in other churches for the first two months. After that, they leased property that Lewis Tappan owned on Pierrepont Street for one dollar per year and held worship services in a temporary building they called a "tabernacle." It was a "primitive" structure, made of the pews and doors of the old church on Cranberry Street and "covered by a vast roof sustained by rude joists and timbers."[31] The cornerstone of the new building was laid on May 29, 1849. Construction was completed in seven

months, and opening services were held in the new meetinghouse on the first Sunday in January 1850.

Despite the difficult circumstances and the absence of Beecher for two months due to illness, the Plymouth membership continued to grow, increasing in 1849 by 125 new members to a total membership of 327.[32]

At the time it was opened, Plymouth Church's new meetinghouse was the largest auditorium in Brooklyn. As a result, it enhanced the outreach of the church. Many people came to hear Beecher. Outside organizations sought to use it for public meetings. Antislavery societies held meetings there. It is likely that the interior design of the space had an impact on those attending. The semicircular design of the pews created relationships among the people in the pews. Wherever an individual was sitting, the person could see and be seen by other people across the room. Being aware of one another, the congregation or audience could, and likely did, experience shared moments of community that resulted in increased participation.

Plymouth's 1850 meetinghouse design influenced interior church architecture. Jeanne Halgren Kilde has shown that the Broadway Tabernacle design influenced the "auditorium style" of Protestant churches built in the 1880s, featuring a prominent stage from which rows of pews radiated up a sloping floor.[33] Plymouth Church's interior architecture was likely the link between Finney's innovative design of 1836 and the later churches. In 1859, the Broadway Tabernacle was moved to an uptown Manhattan location and a new Gothic structure, so that it no longer served as a model for church interior architecture. When this occurred, Plymouth Church remained the most notable and best-known example of Finney design features.

Opposite, top: Interior of Plymouth Church today, showing features that Reverend Beecher specified. The speaking platform thrusts into the congregation, with the pews surrounding it. As at revivals, Beecher wanted to be in the center of a crowd, with people around him. On the stage, he had a lectern rather than a pulpit confining him, placing a barrier between him and his congregation. The room, with sweeping curves, provided excellent acoustics, so everyone could hear. The organ casework and display pipes are from the 1866 E. & G. G. Hook Organ Company. *Author's collection.*

Opposite, bottom: Façade of Plymouth Church on Orange Street, designed by architect Joseph Collins Wells. He had designed Henry Bowen's summer residence in Woodstock, Connecticut, built in 1846. Bowen, a church trustee, probably recommended hiring Wells. Born in England, Wells practiced in Manhattan from 1839 to 1860 and was a founder of the American Institute of Architects. He had designed First Presbyterian Church on Fifth Avenue at Twelfth Street in Manhattan in Gothic Revival style, built in 1844–46. *Collection of Plymouth Church.*

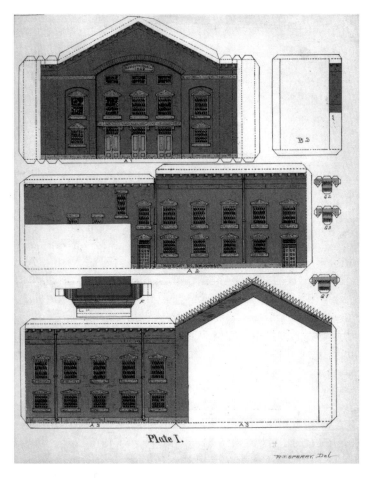

Demonstrating that Plymouth Church was well known in 1882, this color lithograph print model of the church structure was used as an advertisement for Travelers Insurance Company. This page, with a cutout of the Orange Street façade of the meetinghouse, was one of five pages of the model. There were two other pages of cutouts, a page of the instructions and a page of the history of Plymouth Church to be pasted on the bottom of the model. *Collection of Plymouth Church.*

The new meetinghouse gave Plymouth Church a splendid base of operations for helping people to escape from slavery, as Beecher and members and friends of the congregation became "conductors" on the Underground Railroad.

CHAPTER 2

HELPING FUGITIVES ESCAPE
TO FREEDOM

Most people fleeing to freedom traveled north, following, as it was said, the North Star. They had to move away from the slave states to avoid capture by their masters or so-called slave catchers employed by masters pursuing them. Frederick Douglass said that he had a motto on his way from slavery: "Trust no man!" This meant to him, "I saw in every white man an enemy, and in almost every colored man cause for distrust." Yet, for him and for others seeking freedom, it was "a most painful situation" because he and they needed shelter, food and other help.[34]

Many people did help. From the early 1800s, Quakers living in Pennsylvania and New Jersey were known to be "friends" to the self-emancipated people seeking freedom. In later years, other people assisted. When railroads were introduced in the 1830s, the network of people aiding those escaping adopted the language of the railroads and became known as the "Underground Railroad." It employed railroad terminology to describe what was happening. Those fleeing were called "passengers," those escorting were called "conductors," places where fugitives stayed were "stations" and places where many fugitives traveled to freedom were "depots."

Map of major eastern routes of the Underground Railroad through Brooklyn and New York City. Charles Ray called New York "a kind of receiving depot, whence we forwarded to Albany, Troy, and sometimes to New Bedford and Boston, and occasionally we dropped a few on Long Island, when we considered it safe so to do." *Map by Anne Decker, based on information from Wilbur Siebert's* Underground Railroad *and Alexander Flick's* History of the State of New York.

A Dangerous Place for Black People

A common route of travel for those seeking freedom from the slave states of Delaware, Maryland and Virginia was through New York City. As a major harbor, the city also attracted enslaved people fleeing from more distant southern ports by ship. New York City, however, was a dangerous place for fugitives. Since the "Empire City" was a financial and mercantile center, many southerners traveled there to do their banking and shopping. Merchants did a brisk business selling imported goods, including Paris fashions, when southerners made their periodic shopping trips to New York. Also, New York businessmen and bankers were deeply involved in southern products. New York dominated all phases of the cotton trade from plantation to market, including advances for planting new crops through shipping bales to markets. It was estimated that forty cents of every dollar paid for cotton ended up in the pockets of New York businessmen. Cotton and tobacco were return cargoes for vessels bringing goods and immigrants from Europe to New York.[35]

So also, slave catchers came to New York charged to find, capture and bring back to their masters' enslaved persons who had fled there. Until 1850, these men were authorized under the federal Fugitive Slave Law of 1793, which Congress passed to enforce the United States Constitution provision that "no person held to service or labor in one state, under the laws thereof, escaping into another, shall, in consequence of any law or regulation therein, be discharged from such service or labor, but shall be delivered up on claim of the party to whom such service or labor may be due."[36] In 1850, the Fugitive Slave Law was strengthened.

New York was also a dangerous place for free blacks. When slave catchers found free black people, they sometimes kidnapped them, brought them south and sold them to slave traders. It did not matter to these slave catchers if the black people they captured were legally free rather than the fugitives they were commissioned to find.

Committee of Vigilance in the 1830s

In 1835, a group calling itself the New York Committee of Vigilance became the first organization in the United States for the purpose, as committee member Reverend Charles Bennett Ray said, of helping "any colored person who may be arrested upon pretense of being an escaping slave." This included preventing the act of kidnapping free blacks.

> *But our first and practical business is, to take charge of all escaping slaves who may either be sent to us or may try to find us, and to seek out all who may come within our notice to clothe them if need be and to hurry them away with the least possible delay and the greatest speed to a land of safety, paying their passages and giving them letters of introduction to other friends of the cause in other sections of the country, and then in the speediest manner, placing them where the slave pursuer can neither find nor molest them, and where they can be free.* [37]

The secretary of the Committee of Vigilance was David Ruggles, born a free black man in Lyme, Connecticut, in 1810. Moving to New York City at age sixteen, he worked as a mariner and opened a grocery store and then a bookstore. He edited the *Mirror of Liberty*. As secretary of the Committee of Vigilance, he directed the committee's operations. He even maintained a list of slave catchers who were in town and published it so that they could be more easily avoided. When his conduct was questioned and he resigned in 1839, the committee lost some of the assertiveness that it had had when he was leading it. [38]

The committee was primarily an activity of African Americans, although Lewis Tappan and some other white abolitionists helped out. In the 1830s, Tappan helped David Ruggles. In the 1840s, Tappan recorded in his diary only two cases of his having assisted people fleeing slavery. One person was fleeing from Amos Kendall, former postmaster general of Presidents Jackson and Van Buren. The other was a fugitive from Robert M. Johnson, who had been President Van Buren's vice president. [39]

A New Vigilance Committee

In 1847, a group of blacks and whites formed a new committee, the New York State Vigilance Committee. Isaac Hopper, a Quaker known as the "father of the Underground Railroad," was its president. In 1848, the committee was reorganized with Gerrit Smith from upstate New York as its president and

Reverend Charles B. Ray. *Author's collection.*

Charles Ray from New York City as its corresponding secretary, a position he had held in the earlier Committee of Vigilance. Ray was born a free man in Falmouth, Massachusetts, in 1807. After studying theology at Wesleyan Seminary in Wilbraham, Massachusetts, he enrolled as the first black student at Wesleyan University in Middletown, Connecticut, but his enrollment was revoked less than two months later after white students protested. He was ordained and served as pastor of two predominately white churches in New York City, Crosby Congregational Church and Bethesda Congregational Church. He and Lewis Tappan taught Sunday school together. From 1838 to 1841, Ray was an owner and editor of the weekly periodical *Colored American*.[40]

When Charles Ray became director of the committee's operations, his longtime friend and colleague Lewis Tappan became active in committee work in several ways. For one, Tappan helped raise money. Plymouth Church member Anthony Lane, who had been a clerk at the dry goods store of Arthur and Lewis Tappan, was treasurer of the committee for many years. Lane said that because of Tappan's extensive correspondence abroad—especially for the American and Foreign Anti-Slavery Society, with its close ties to members of the British and Foreign Anti-Slavery Society—many contributions to the vigilance committee came from England and Scotland. Indeed, on one occasion, an "extensive invoice of useful and fancy articles, in several large boxes, was received from Glasgow ladies, sufficient to furnish a large bazaar or fair, which was held in Brooklyn, for the benefit of the committee."[41]

As a second way, he often received information about slave catchers and acted on it. For instance, a black man came to his home and asked Tappan to alert a fugitive that the slave owner was in the city looking for him. Tappan found the man, warned him and allowed him to avoid capture. Sometimes, information about those pursuing fugitives came through his wide correspondence. On one occasion, he received word that an officer from Savannah, Georgia, was heading north to find two young men who were nineteen or twenty years old. Tappan immediately notified African American churches and Sunday schools. When he talked with Charles Ray, who was a school superintendent, Ray identified one of the young men. That person located the other, and they both "put themselves out of harm's way," as Tappan told it.[42]

In addition, Lane said that Tappan was "almost always at their meetings, which were known only to 'the elect,' for we dared not hold them too publicly, as we almost always had some of the travelers toward the 'north star' present, whose masters or their agents were frequently in the city, in hot pursuit."[43]

They dared not hold their meetings too publicly for good reason: they were discussing how to violate federal law. Under the Fugitive Slave Law of 1793 and, later, under the revised law of 1850, persons helping fugitives escape from slavery, if found liable, could be penalized. The 1793 law provided that a person could be held liable for a $500 penalty (in 2012 dollars, it would be $15,000). Under the 1850 law, the penalty was more severe.

Opposing slavery and helping fugitives escape from slavery was a dangerous activity. Those opposed to the abolitionists organized mobs that became violent. In the 1834 anti-abolitionist riots in New York City, a mob attacked Arthur and Lewis Tappan's store. The twenty-year-old Henry Bowen, a new Tappan employee, helped defend the store from the approaching mob with other clerks, armed with guns. At the same time, a mob broke into Lewis Tappan's home and burned the family's furnishings in the street in front of the house. Fortunately, Tappan and his wife and children were elsewhere.

Nevertheless, those seeking help knew how to locate people who would help. Thus, one summer morning, there was a loud knock on the front door of Charles Ray's home. A black man entered and asked, "Does Reverend Mr. Ray live here?" When he received an affirmative answer, he whistled and cried out, "Come on, boys!" and fourteen fugitive men entered the house.[44]

Also, one morning, when Lewis Tappan came to work at the American Missionary Association, he found eighteen fugitive men, women and children who were, as he said, "lying about on the bales and boxes of clothing destined for our various missionary stations, fatigued, as they doubtless were, after their sleepless and protracted struggle for freedom." They had come from a southern city to Philadelphia and across New Jersey to his office. He arranged for them to go to Albany and thereafter to Canada.[45]

Ray and Tappan joined the work of the vigilance committee with that of the antislavery office. Ray said, "An indispensable auxiliary to the work of the Vigilance Committee was the Underground Railroad."[46] In

William Still. *Author's collection.*

Washington, D.C., they worked with several people, in addition to William Chaplin, who helped the Edmonsons. Also in Washington was Gamaliel Bailey, whom Tappan from the antislavery office had persuaded to leave Cincinnati to become editor of the newspaper *National Era*.

In Philadelphia, William Still was the coordinator of the antislavery activities. Born in Burlington, New Jersey, in 1821, Still moved to Philadelphia in 1844 and worked as a clerk for the Pennsylvania Society for the Abolition of Slavery. When the society created a committee to aid runaways from slavery, he became its chairman. He helped as many as sixty people per month escape slavery, interviewing each person and keeping careful records of biographies and destinations of people coming through his office. After the Civil War, he published his records as a book entitled *The Underground Railroad*.

In addition to helping fugitives from slavery, the New York State Vigilance Committee on a number of occasions sought to free enslaved servants who were brought to New York by their owners. In 1817, the New York legislature had banned importation of enslaved people into the state and, in 1841, had repealed the law that permitted out-of-state owners to bring their servants with them through the state for a nine-month period. The best known of the committee's cases was the *Lemmon* case. In November 1852, Virginians Jonathan Lemmon and his wife brought with them eight enslaved servants and their children between the ages of two and twenty-three for the purpose of catching a ship to Texas, where they planned to live. While waiting for the ship, the Lemmons housed the servants and children in a boardinghouse, where Louis Napoleon, a free black man, learned about them. The committee arranged for Napoleon, who was illiterate, to bring a writ of habeas corpus to obtain their freedom. Judge Elijah Paine of the Superior Court of New York City held that they were free under state law.[47]

THE GRAND CENTRAL DEPOT OF THE UNDERGROUND RAILROAD

Sometimes, the committee needed to hide people in Brooklyn. Ray reported that he delivered "several" fugitives to Plymouth Church. The Plymouth congregation gave benevolence moneys to Ray for helping free enslaved blacks. In addition, the church had sources other than the vigilance committee for helping people fleeing slavery. Abolitionists in southern states directed fleeing enslaved persons to go to Henry Ward Beecher. He had an arrangement with Louis Napoleon that, when an enslaved person was sent to him or the church, Napoleon would "fix things along the Central Railroad and see to it that the officials along the route were got into friendly disposition for the fugitive." The *Brooklyn Daily Eagle* reported that "dozens passed through Mr. Beecher's hands in this way." In one of his sermons, Beecher said of fugitive enslaved people, "I will both shelter them, conceal them, or speed their flight; and while under my shelter, or under my convoy, they shall be to me as my own flesh and blood; and whatever defense I would put forth for my own children, that shall these poor, despised creatures have in my house or upon the road." Church tradition states that fugitives were harbored in the basement of the church. A Plymouth Church historian called Plymouth "the Grand Central Depot of the Underground Railroad."[48]

In upstate New York, the vigilance committee had contacts with several antislavery people and organizations. In the late 1840s, Reverend Henry Highland Garnet, an American Missionary Association Executive Committee member, was pastor of the Liberty Street Presbyterian Church in Troy and assisted fugitives. Garnet had been born in slavery in Maryland, but when he was nine years old, he and his family escaped to New York City, where his father proclaimed his family free and renamed each member. He completed his schooling at the Oneida Institute in Whitesboro, New York, where Lewis Tappan's sons had gone to school at Charles Grandison Finney's suggestion.

Gerrit Smith, the vigilance committee president, lived in Peterboro, located south of Oneida, and ran an Underground Railroad site. As the result of his father's longtime partnership with John Jacob Astor and his mother being a member of the Livingston family, Smith owned a vast amount of land in upper New York State. He decided to make gifts of plots of land in North Elba, near Lake Placid, to blacks so that they would have farms and would meet the property requirement for voting under New York law. He chose Charles Ray, Dr. James McCune Smith and Reverend Theodore Wright as his trustees to distribute the

Above: Basement of Plymouth Church. *Collection of Plymouth Church.*

Left: This photograph of Gerrit Smith was taken between 1855 and 1865. *Brady-Handy Photograph Collection, Library of Congress.*

land. Smith's close friend Frederick Douglass participated in the Underground Railroad in Rochester. The American Missionary Association, of which Ray and Tappan were leaders, supported missionaries at Amherstburgh, Mount Hope, St. Catherine's, New Canaan, Windsor and several other locations to help refugees in Canada West, now called Ontario.[49]

THE WEEMS FAMILY ESCAPES FROM SLAVERY

The extent and effectiveness of the network described here is well demonstrated by the saga of the eight-year quest for freedom of the Weems family of Rockville, Maryland.[50] John Weems was a free black man, but his wife, Arrah, was enslaved, and therefore their three daughters and three sons were, too. In 1850, one daughter, Stella, ran away with her aunt and uncle to upstate New York. Arrah's master promised to allow John to purchase the freedom of his wife and their family. When Arrah's master died, John set out to raise the needed money. In 1852, he traveled to New York City, where he met with Charles Ray of the vigilance committee. Using the antislavery network, Ray located Stella's aunt and uncle in Canada West and learned that Stella had gone to England as the "adopted daughter" of Reverend Garnet, who was to lecture there. When John returned home, he discovered that Arrah and their children were in the Washington jail pending sale to slave traders and learned that it would cost him $3,300 ($101,000 in 2012 dollars) to purchase their freedom. That presented a huge challenge, as in the case of the Edmonson sisters.

Ray made things easier almost immediately. He asked Garnet to "solicit a little assistance" from the English. Garnet persuaded Quaker abolitionists Henry and Anna Richardson to raise money. Eventually, they raised $5,000. Based on this, Washington lawyer Jacob Bigelow started negotiating with the slave trader, Charles M. Price, in March 1853. When Price demanded $1,000 for thirteen-year-old daughter Ann Maria, Bigelow and Ray decided that the amount was too high for a girl of her age, so they concluded that they had "to run her off."

Price was worried that Ann Maria would try to escape, so he had her sleep in the same room with him and his wife. On September 23, 1855, Ann Maria managed to leave Price's house. Because Price offered a $500 reward for her, she hid with black families "until the storm passed." Finally,

two months later, William Still sent a Philadelphia college professor, called "Dr. H.," to escort her from Washington. On November 22, Bigelow walked with Ann Maria, disguised as a boy, to a carriage near the White House. She climbed in and pretended to be Dr. H.'s driver until they passed the city limits. They stopped at the house of a Maryland slave owner, where Dr. H. introduced Ann Maria as his slave, "Little Boy Joe." When they arrived in Philadelphia, Ann Maria went to William Still's home. There, Still took her picture dressed as a boy.

Still sent her on to New York City, where she first stayed with Charles Ray and then with Lewis Tappan. She spent Thanksgiving at the Tappans' house in Brooklyn as the family entertained guests

MARIA WEEMS ESCAPING IN MALE ATTIRE.

Top: Reverend Henry Highland Garnet. *Author's collection.*

Bottom: Ann Maria Weems, shown disguised by cutting her hair and wearing the attire of a male carriage driver, in woodcut based on the photograph taken by William Still. *Manuscripts, Archives and Rare Books Division, Schomburg Center for Research in Black Culture, the New York Public Library, Astor, Lenox and Tilden Foundations.*

below and family members delivered dinner to her in an upper-floor room. On the next day, Tappan took her to Reverend Freeman, the black pastor of Siloam Presbyterian Church in Brooklyn. Born in Rahway, New Jersey, Freeman had studied at the Oneida Institute in Whitesboro, New York, and moved to Portland, Maine, where he was ordained and became pastor of the Fourth Congregational Church. Freeman agreed to take Ann Maria to her aunt and uncle in Canada. They left on the five o'clock afternoon train, with Freeman worried that, since there was a large reward on her, there might be "some lurking spy ready to pounce upon us." The trip was uneventful. They crossed the suspension bridge to Canada West, and at an early stop, Ann Maria changed her clothes to those of a girl, shedding her disguise. Finally, two days later, she joined her aunt and uncle.[51]

Over time, Arrah, the Weemses' one other daughter and their three sons all had their freedom purchased. Arrah Weems participated in freeing their sons. In addition, she became a conductor of the Underground Railroad when she rescued a fourteen-month-old boy as a part of a fundraising trip throughout the North. Finally, their last child was freed in August 1858.

Even though violating federal law, the vigilance committee issued to the public fundraising circulars and annual reports that reveal some of the numbers of people assisted by its work from 1847 to 1860. An 1849 handwritten fundraising circular for the executive board by William Harned of the Plymouth Church community, Charles Ray and Andrew Lester noted that over the previous fifteen months, the vigilance committee had assisted more than 400 persons in escaping from slavery. The 1850 annual report of the committee noted that its members had assisted 151 fugitives in the year from May 1849. According to its 1853 annual report, the committee assisted 686 former enslaved persons from January 1851 to April 1853. Between 1851 and 1853, the committee successfully sued to free 38 blacks who had been brought to New York by their slaveholders, such as the eight people freed in the *Lemmon* case. The vigilance committee continued its work afterward, although we do not know about annual reports after 1853. In 1857, Lewis Tappan wrote that the vigilance committee "makes good use of the funds committed to it. Every week almost fugitives arrive here in destitute circumstances."[52]

The success of the New York State Vigilance Committee in helping fugitives from slavery gain freedom became a problem, as it caused southerners to seek to persuade Congress to strengthen laws to aid them in preventing escapes from slavery.

CHAPTER 3

THE FUGITIVE SLAVE LAW

On July 18, 1850, during Congressional debates over strengthening the federal Fugitive Slave Law, Seth Barton, a New Orleans lawyer writing under the pseudonym "Randolph of Roanoke," published a pamphlet arguing that by "enticing" enslaved people to escape, northerners had caused southern property losses over the previous forty years of $22 million (in 2012 dollars, it would be $667 million).

In recent years, Barton said, northerners had acted "through organized associations, with alarming frequency and a most amazing audacity." The example he cited was the New York State Vigilance Committee. Two months earlier, the committee had held its annual meeting "in public" in New York City. He quoted the committee's annual report noting that, within the year since May 1, 1849, it had "assisted one hundred and fifty-one fugitives (for that, you know, is our business) in escaping from servitude!" He asserted, "One of the worst omens of the times is, the shamelessness with which of late, men of property and character at the North, avow and boast of their criminal participation in decoying away and depriving owners of their slaves in the slave States."[53]

Six months before Barton issued his pamphlet, Virginia senator James Mason had introduced a bill "for the more effectual execution" of the Fugitive Slave Law. South Carolina senator Andrew P. Butler, chairman of the Judiciary Committee that had favorably reported the bill, opened by saying that he had "very little confidence" that the bill would accomplish its purpose. For years, southerners had been trying to strengthen the Fugitive Slave Law of 1793, but to no avail.

SENATOR CLAY'S PROPOSED COMPROMISE

Daguerreotype of Senator Henry Clay of Kentucky taken by Mathew Brady between 1850 and 1852. *Library of Congress.*

Five days after Butler made his statement, however, possibilities for passage improved. Kentucky senator Henry Clay, known as the "Great Pacificator" for having brokered important compromises, proposed eight bills, including a provision for a tougher Fugitive Slave Law. He described his proposal as a "great national scheme of compromise and harmony."[54]

The compromise was needed because of issues raised by the treaty that ended the Mexican-American War. The treaty gave the United States the Rio Grande boundary for Texas, as well as the land that became the states of California, Nevada and Utah, most of Arizona and New Mexico and parts of Wyoming and Colorado. Congressmen expected that when they convened in December 1849, they would decide how to organize the new federal territories. However, before Congress met, Californians had drafted and approved a free-state constitution, elected a governor and two senators and petitioned for statehood. By so doing, they had bypassed the territorial stage altogether.

Southerners had reason to be concerned if California were admitted as a free state. In the preceding decades, with southern slave states having at least the same number of senators as northern free states had, the southern senators could block any legislation adversely affecting the status of slavery. Now, however, if California became the thirty-first state, slavery would be barred in sixteen states and legal in only fifteen.

In Senator Clay's proposed compromise, he tried to give something to everyone. His eight bills were made up of two pairs relating to the western territories, each part of a pair being intended to appeal to either the North or the South, and three bills concerning slavery in the District of Columbia. On the grounds that the other seven resolutions were more favorable to the North than to the South, he offered the South a strengthened Fugitive Slave Law.

Senator Clay's proposed compromise was made against the background of southern threats of secession. In January 1850, the *New York Journal of Commerce* reported that if Congress enacted laws restricting slavery in federal territories, a secession movement would sweep the South. Starting then and continuing through the spring, the paper printed extracts of letters from southerners addressed to New York merchants, telling them that purchases for the spring trade would be delayed or not made at all because of the sectional disputes. Since southerners had purchased more than $76 million ($2.35 billion in 2012 dollars) of merchandise in New York in 1849, the letters commanded attention.[55]

Senator Clay argued that compromise was necessary to save the Union. Henry Ward Beecher disagreed, explaining that even though some people were convinced that "no evil can be so great as the dissolution of our Union," many evils are "infinitely greater." He said that the "loss of public humanity is greater." As applied to slavery, "an indifference to the condition of millions of miserable" enslaved people would be "an unspeakably greater evil."[56]

Plymouth Church Members Oppose Compromise

In the following months, members of the Plymouth Church community Joshua Leavitt, Henry Bowen, Henry Ward Beecher and Lewis Tappan opposed the compromise.

In numerous unsigned articles, the *Independent*'s managing editor, Joshua Leavitt, vigorously attacked the proposal to strengthen the Fugitive Slave Law. In this connection, the paper advised its readers to aid fugitives with food, clothing, shelter, money and protection while avoiding violence. The idea of a "Higher Law" was the basis of many of its opinions. The newspaper defined the Higher Law as "a rule of right and wrong above the Constitution and above the Sovereignty of the Union—a law eternal and unchangeable—which no legislation can violate without guilt."[57]

Bowen, a proprietor of the *Independent*, had arranged for Beecher to write articles for the paper. Beecher wrote several articles about the compromise. Regarding the Fugitive Slave Law, he declared that he would not be bound by any compromise that required people to "violate humanity." He said that he would not help recapturing a "fellow man for bondage." He insisted, "Not even the Constitution shall make me unjust." In this connection, he asserted the Higher Law doctrine, saying, "If asked, what becomes of the Constitution, I reply by asking what becomes of God's Constitution of Humanity, if you give back a slave to the remorseless maw of servitude? I put Constitution against Constitution—God's against man's. Where they agree they are doubly sacred. Where they differ my reply to all questioners, but especially to all timid Christian scruples, is in the language of Peter: 'Whether it be right, in the sight of God, to hearken unto you more than unto God, judge ye.'"[58]

Samuel Ringgold Ward, born enslaved and a fugitive from slavery and later a vice-president of the American Missionary Association, recognized Henry Ward Beecher's unique contribution to the advocacy of freedom. In his 1855 *Autobiography of a Fugitive Negro*, Ward singled out Beecher for praise as an honor to his profession—"the bold, the honest, the self-sacrificing, the amiable Henry Ward Beecher." Ward did not refer to specific incidents. Since Ward had fled the United States to go to Canada in 1851, his comments most likely referred to Beecher's activities before that, including his strong affirmation of the Higher Law doctrine in opposition to the Fugitive Slave Law.[59]

New York senator William H. Seward was criticized for arguing Higher Law in his March 11 speech in the Senate. By contrast, Beecher continued to make arguments against the Fugitive Slave Bill based on the violations of Higher Law. Later, Beecher advised his readers that "every citizen must obey a law which inflicts injury upon his person, estate, and civil privilege, until legally redressed; but no citizen is bound to obey a law which commands *him* to inflict injury upon another."[60] In addition, in November 1850, Henry's brother, Charles, delivered a sermon on the Fugitive Slave Law entitled

Opposite: Samuel Ringgold Ward. *Author's collection.*

Left: Photographic print of Senator William H. Seward of New York. *Library of Congress.*

"The Duty of Disobedience to Wicked Laws," discussing the Higher Law doctrine at length.

Lewis Tappan went to Washington to help organize opposition to Clay's compromise. He was present in March when great speeches were made. In his famous speech of March 7, Massachusetts senator Daniel Webster supported the compromise. Tappan, who heard the speech, wrote to British abolitionists, "To the astonishment of the country Daniel Webster now came forward in the Senate as the advocate of Southern interests, in total disregard of the declarations made by him for a series of years." Tappan commented, "What a fall for D. Webster! He seems to have lost his moral sense." Tappan helped New Hampshire senator John P. Hale write a reply to Webster's support of the compromise.[61]

Although memorable, the speeches did not convince the Senate to pass Clay's bills. So, in April, Clay secured the appointment of a Select

Senator Daniel Webster of Massachusetts, shown addressing the Senate in the Old Senate Chamber on March 7, 1850, during the debate over the Compromise of 1850. Each member of the 1850 Senate is depicted in this print, created in about 1860. *Library of Congress.*

Committee of Thirteen to consider his and other proposals that had been made. In May, Clay reported the conclusions of the Select Committee. The major suggestion was to incorporate all the subjects that had been proposed into a single bill. President Zachary Taylor mocked the idea of a single bill by calling it an "omnibus bill," a vehicle on which any provision could ride.

ANTISLAVERY SOCIETIES MEETINGS

While Clay was reporting for the Select Committee, antislavery societies were holding annual meetings in New York City. New York merchants opposed holding the meetings if antislavery issues would be discussed. They feared that their southern customers would be angered if they learned what was said. The *New York Globe* exclaimed, "No public buildings, not even the streets must be desecrated by such a proposed assemblage of traitors."[62]

In addition, gangs of "b'hoys" or "rowdies" supported by the Democratic Party sought to disrupt the meetings so that "no business could be done."

Left: William Lloyd Garrison. *Library of Congress.*

Right: This daguerreotype of Wendell Phillips was taken by Mathew Brady between 1853 and 1860. *Library of Congress.*

The term "b'hoy," derived from the Irish pronunciation of the word "boy," became popular in New York City in the 1840s after theatrical productions portrayed workers who were characterized by their red shirts, heavy boots and boisterousness and were also called "rowdies" or "roughs." They targeted the meetings of William Lloyd Garrison's American Anti-Slavery Society, the Boston-based antislavery organization. Captain Isaiah Rynders, a colorful gambler and knife fighter as well as the Tammany Hall ward boss of Five Points, led a gang to disrupt the meetings. According to the *Brooklyn Daily Eagle*, the meetings "have been attended by gangs of rowdies and bullies, who have disturbed the speakers in all possible ways; by whistling, calling for 'niggers,' giving the lie to the speaker, and creating such a storm of hideous noises."[63]

At the meeting of the American and Foreign Anti-Slavery Society, Lewis Tappan said there had been "some little disturbance." However, he said, "no serious interruption took place." Beecher spoke at Tappan's meeting. He experienced some heckling. He spoke about slavery, saying that slaveholders needed "to keep men brutal." He asserted, "The slave is made just good enough to be a slave, and no more. It is a penitentiary offense to teach him more." A heckler interrupted by shouting, "It is a lie!" Beecher, with humor, responded by saying, "Well, whether it is a penitentiary offense or not, I will not argue with the gentleman. Doubtless he has been there, and ought to know." After laughter and applause, Beecher continued with his speech.[64]

In contrast with Beecher's experience, Wendell Phillips, a noted speaker called "abolition's golden trumpet," did not get an opportunity to address the meeting of the American Anti-Slavery Society because of the antics of the b'hoys. When he learned that Phillips would not be heard, Beecher arranged with Plymouth Church's trustees to have Phillips speak at the new meetinghouse.

DOUGLAS RESCUES THE BILL

On July 4, President Taylor, who opposed Senator Clay's bill, died suddenly. Vice President Millard Fillmore, a New Yorker with southern sympathies, became president. Shortly afterward, he let it be known that he supported the compromise. The promised support of the president was not enough, however, to secure the passage of Clay's omnibus bill. On July 31, the bill came up for a vote. As an omnibus bill, it was complex, having provisions that appealed to senators but also provisions that they disliked, and it went down in defeat. Some of the credit for persuading senators to vote against the bill was the result of the work of abolitionists, including those from Plymouth Church. After six months, Clay's attempt to orchestrate a compromise had failed. Disappointed and fatigued, Clay left Washington to go to Newport, Rhode Island, to recover.

At this point, Illinois senator Stephen A. Douglas stepped forward to manage the compromise proposals. Many of the bills had initially come through his Committee on Territories. He separated the omnibus bill into its various parts. Then he proceeded to organize support from various groups of senators for each of the individual bills. Abolitionists organized opposition to the Fugitive Slave Bill. On August 21 and 22, they held a notable convention at Cazenovia, New York, but that did not prevent its passage. In a remarkable exercise of political and parliamentary tactics, Senator Douglas shepherded

This daguerreotype was taken at the Fugitive Slave Bill convention at Cazenovia, New York. Gerrit Smith has his hand raised. Mary Edmonson is to his right, with Emily to his left. Charles Ray is to the left of the man standing behind the man writing at the table. Frederick Douglass is at the right end of the table, with Theodore Weld sitting in front of him. Theodore's brother, Ezra Greenleaf Weld, took the daguerreotype, which presented a laterally reversed image. *From the Collection of the Madison County Historical Society, Oneida, New York.*

each of the bills through the Senate and, thereafter, provided leadership to secure support in the House. By September 18, President Fillmore had signed each of the bills, and they had become law.

The individual bills except the Fugitive Slave Law ceased to be controversial as soon as President Fillmore signed them. On December 14, Georgians meeting in convention approved what was called the "Georgia Platform." While they did "not wholly approve" the compromise, they said that they would "abide by it as a permanent adjustment of this sectional controversy." They went on to state that "upon a faithful execution" of the law "depends the preservation of our much beloved Union."[65] This platform became southern policy for the next several years.

At public meetings in city after city in the North, people proclaimed their hostility to the law and opposition to enforcement. At its September annual meeting, the American Missionary Association, for which Lewis Tappan helped make policy, took the position that simply stated, "We cannot obey it." The law was "at variance" with the association, the United States Constitution and the law of God.[66]

As the law was enacted, northerners had four basic complaints. First, in legal proceedings, the fugitive was not entitled to any individual rights, due process or jury trial. Indeed, the fugitive's testimony would not be admitted. A substantial risk existed that free blacks in the North would be "kidnapped" and sent to the South on no evidence other than a claim, without a chance to present a defense.

Second, northerners thought that the act provided for excessively severe penalties. Persons who gave shelter, food or assistance to an escaping person were liable to be fined $1,000 and imprisoned for six months. In addition, the act provided a civil penalty of $1,000.

Third, the law provided for the appointment of special commissioners to handle cases. The commissioners were paid ten dollars for every person they returned to slavery but only five dollars for every person they determined to be free. Northerners argued that this acted as a bribe. These provisions were odious enough, according to Henry Ward Beecher, "to render an infamous thing consistently infamous throughout."[67]

Finally and most controversial, the law commanded citizens "to aid and assist in the prompt and efficient execution of this law, whenever their services may be required." This provision was a significant mistake by southern strategists. They should have allowed northerners to ignore the law. As it was, the federal government required every American to become a slave catcher.

JAMES HAMLET: FIRST PERSON ARRESTED

Southern slave owners sent their agents north as soon as the bill became law. Ten days after the law was signed, thirty-year-old James Hamlet, a porter in New York City with a wife and two children, became the first person to be arrested under the new law. Lewis Tappan apparently tried to help Hamlet during the hearing before the commissioner. Tappan identified a person he described as "a gentleman who has some sympathy for the distressed." This person arrived at the hearing "by accident," saw what was happening and then sent for a lawyer. The lawyer appeared in time to cross-examine the witnesses.

In a pamphlet Tappan wrote about the case, he suggested that Hamlet had been captured and sent to Maryland under false pretenses. Hamlet, he said, "insisted that his mother was a free woman, and that he was a free man, and denied he was a slave." But the law prohibited his testimony, and he was not heard.[68]

The case aroused indignation even among New York merchants who supported the law. Hamlet's employers wrote the slave owner, asking to purchase Hamlet's freedom. When she set a price of $800, they contributed and appealed to the *Journal of Commerce* to solicit from other merchants.

At the close of the October 2 meeting to raise money, Charles Ray arrived and announced that the money had been raised. Lewis Tappan helped raise the money. Upon Hamlet's arrival in New York on Saturday, October 5, a "great demonstration" of four to five thousand people occurred. After his return, Hamlet resumed his job as a porter.

In its report of the *Hamlet* case, the *Brooklyn Daily Eagle* described "excitement" within the black community. The paper noted that the excitement was understandable because there were "many negroes in this vicinity who stand in similar circumstances" as Hamlet. In other articles at that time, the *Daily Eagle* wrote about "excitement" in Philadelphia, Harrisburg, Detroit and Pittsburgh.[69]

NEW YORK MERCHANTS ORGANIZE

When the Fugitive Slave Law was enacted, southern customers informed New York merchants that the law must be enforced. They convinced the merchants that to keep their southern customers happy, they would have to persuade other northerners to enforce the law.

On October 23, the merchants announced that they would have a meeting at the Castle Garden to organize a rally to show their support for the law. Within a week, ten thousand merchants had signed up to support the meeting. When a small number of firms refused to sign the call, the organizers created a "blacklist" of merchants with whom southerners should not do business. The *New York Day Book* printed the names of eight firms that had rejected the call, characterizing them as "Abolitionists." The *Day Book* also sent the list of names to southern newspapers, urging southerners to "shun these fanatics" and "drop them like a viper." Beecher visited the blacklisted merchants to express his support and to encourage them.[70]

Henry Bowen and his business partner Thomas McNamee were among those who refused to sign the call. The *Journal of Commerce* attacked the firm in its columns. Bowen asked Beecher to assist him in drafting a "card" or business advertisement for the newspapers. Beecher suggested that the main idea should be, "My goods are for sale, but not my principles."[71]

"Our goods, and not our principles, are in the market" became a rallying cry for antislavery businessmen. Bowen and McNamee's action was recognized as demonstrating rare courage among New York merchants. Western and northern merchants were encouraged to patronize Bowen and McNamee to compensate them for the loss of southern customers.[72]

The editors of the *Independent* defended Bowen and McNamee's stand, stating that the Fugitive Slave Law was evil. The *Independent*'s position was attacked in New York City by other religious newspapers and by secular papers like the *Journal of Commerce*. As a result of its editorial position, the *Independent* lost about a half of its six thousand subscribers but gained five thousand new ones. This marked a shift in the audience of the newspaper and allowed the editors to continue its antislavery editorials.[73]

Also as a result of the *Independent*'s editorial position, one of the five original proprietors, Simeon Chittenden, asked to have his ownership share purchased by the others. After arbitration, his share was purchased in 1853.[74]

On October 30, the Union Meeting took place. According to the *Brooklyn Daily Eagle*, the Castle Garden "was never before so thoroughly filled as it was last night." At the end of the meeting, resolutions relating to the compromise and the Fugitive Slave Law were adopted by acclamation.

At the conclusion of the meeting, one hundred New York merchants resolved to organize what they called the Union Safety Committee to continue the active support of the Union and the law.[75]

Despite these activities, opposition continued. In April 1851, Lewis Tappan remained confident that antislavery forces would be successful. He said that the law was "not popular anywhere" and was "distasteful to the great body of people, especially those who reside in the country towns. It may remain on the statute book but if so it will become a dead letter."[76]

In May 1851, antislavery societies held meetings at which speakers, including Henry Ward Beecher, urged repeal. In Beecher's speech, he also expressed concern for the living conditions of free blacks in the North.

The Union Safety Committee's campaign continued into the fall of 1851. Daniel Webster made speeches in upper New York State. In October 1851, speaking to a group of Syracuse businessmen, he raved that all who dared to oppose the Fugitive Slave Law were "traitors! traitors! traitors!"[77] The campaign worked. After the votes were counted and analyzed, it was apparent that the committee had achieved a substantial success.[78] Candidates supported by them had been elected. Thus, by the fall of 1851, public opposition to the Fugitive Slave Law had declined.

The law, it seemed, was no longer a prominent issue. Northerners had turned their attention to other matters. The so-called compromise seemed to have worked—at least for the moment. What the abolitionists needed was a new burst of energy, a new issue.

As it turned out, Henry Ward Beecher's sister, Harriet Beecher Stowe, would provide increased energy of a different kind.

CHAPTER 4

THE IMPACT OF *UNCLE TOM'S CABIN*

Even though she disliked confrontation, Harriet Beecher Stowe was frustrated by the unwillingness of "good people" to express themselves forcefully against the immorality of slavery and the Fugitive Slave Law. "You don't know how my heart burns within me at the blindness and obtuseness of good people on so very simple a point of morality as this," she told her brother Henry on February 1, 1851. "Some of the defenses of these principles are so very guarded and candid and cautious and sweet and explanatory."[79]

In January 1851, editor Gamaliel Bailey of the *National Era* sent her a letter enclosing one hundred dollars for her to write for his newspaper. He told her that she might write "*as much* as she pleased, *what* she pleased, and *when* she pleased." Harriet had known Bailey for a long time. Graduating from Jefferson

Opposite: Harriet Beecher Stowe. *Collection of Plymouth Church.*

Left: Harriet Beecher Stowe and Henry Ward Beecher pictured in carte de visite style. Their closeness seems to have started after their mother died when Harriet was five years old and Henry was three, and they acted almost as if they were twins, always hand in hand. *Collection of Plymouth Church.*

Medical College in Philadelphia, he moved to Cincinnati, where he practiced medicine and was a lecturer in physiology at Lane Theological Seminary. Despite the printing office being wrecked three times by anti-abolitionist mobs, he edited the antislavery *Philanthropist* from 1836 until he moved to Washington, D.C., to be editor of the *National Era* in 1847.[80]

At first, Harriet did not think about writing about the Fugitive Slave Law. As recently as August, she had written a story about the law. She considered writing "a sketch" for Bailey's paper, describing "the capabilities of liberated blacks to take care of themselves." She wanted to do more about the Fugitive Slave Law, but she thought that she did not have the opportunity. She wrote to Henry that she wished she had his chance to make a difference. Her sister-in-law, Isabella, encouraged her to write about the outrages caused by the Fugitive Slave Law.

Dr. Gamaliel Bailey. This reproduction of a portrait of Dr. Bailey was collected by Ohio State professor Wilbur H. Siebert, whose comprehensive history of the Underground Railroad was published in 1898. *Ohio Historical Society.*

"Now, Hattie," she said, "if I could use a pen as you can, I would write something that would make this whole nation feel what an accursed thing slavery is." One of Harriet's children recalled that, when this letter was read aloud, Harriet "rose up in her chair" and vowed, "I will write something. I will if I live."[81]

A BEST-SELLING NOVEL

By March, Harriet had developed a plan. She wrote to Bailey that she had commenced a story that she described as "a series of sketches which give the lights and shadows of the 'patriarchal institution,'" which was her way of referring to what others called the South's "peculiar institution." She wrote, "My vocation is simply that of *painter*, and my object will be to hold up in the most lifelike and graphic manner possible Slavery, its reverses, changes, and the negro character, which I have had ample opportunities for studying." She told Bailey, "I shall show the *best side* of the thing, and something *faintly approaching the worst*." As she said, "There is no arguing with pictures, and everybody is impressed with them, whether they mean to or not." She later claimed that she had visions of the story, "one after another," and all she did was "put them down in words."[82]

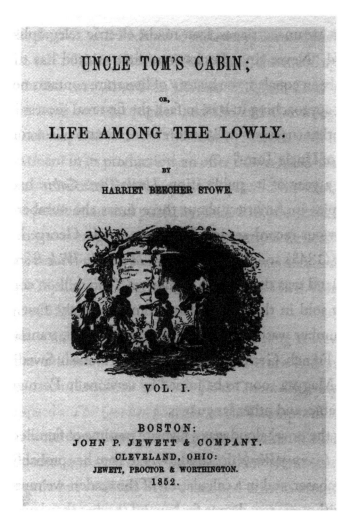

Title page of the first edition of *Uncle Tom's Cabin.* The cabin is the mirror image of a cabin on the right side of the logo design of William Lloyd Garrison's paper, the *Liberator.* The illustrator, Hammatt Billings, was an architect who began his career as an illustrator in the early 1840s for the popular weekly *Gleason's Pictorial Drawing Room Companion. Author's collection.*

Harriet said her "sketches" would be written "either from observation, incidents which have occurred in the sphere of my personal knowledge, or in the knowledge of my friends."[83] She had lived in Cincinnati for eighteen years, from 1832 to 1850. Located across the Ohio River from the slave state of Kentucky, she had learned about slavery from friends and observation. She had visited a Kentucky plantation and had employed as household servants formerly enslaved women who had described their slavery experiences. On one occasion, she and her brother Henry had helped a servant of hers who was a fugitive being sought by slave catchers to escape to the farm of John Van Zandt, an event that became an episode in *Uncle Tom's Cabin.*[84]

The first weekly installment of *Uncle Tom's Cabin* was printed in the *National Era* on June 5, 1851. The story was much longer than the "three or four numbers" she had told Bailey it would run. While missing three deadlines, installments continued for ten months until April 1, 1852.

Ten days before the last installment was published in the *National Era*, John P. Jewett & Company of Boston published *Uncle Tom's Cabin* in two volumes. It quickly became a bestseller. By the end of the first year, 300,000 copies of the novel had been sold in the United States. That was about three times the record for sales of previous novels. Since families and literary groups of that time read books aloud, the book had a larger audience than those who purchased it.

International sales exceeded those in the United States. In the first year, 1 million copies were sold in the United Kingdom. During that year, the book was translated and published in French, German, Spanish, Italian, Danish, Swedish, Flemish, Polish and Magyar. International sales in the first year were over 2 million copies. In later years, it was translated into other languages.

Less than a year after publication of her novel, Harriet described what she thought were the "effects of the book so far." First was "to soften and moderate the bitterness of feeling in *extreme abolitionists*." Second was "to convert to abolitionist views many whom the same bitterness had repelled." Third was "to inspire the free colored people with self-respect, hope, and confidence." And fourth was "to inspire universally through the country a kindlier feeling toward the negro race."[85]

Uncle Tom's Cabin was well received by abolitionists. Lewis Tappan was enthusiastic about it. In his correspondence with representatives of the British and Foreign Anti-Slavery Society, he reported the novel's enthusiastic acceptance. He described the book as "a most interesting work" that has "met with an unprecedented sale & richly deserves it." The American and Foreign Anti-Slavery Society for which he was writing had adopted a resolution at its May 1852 annual meeting, stating that the book was "a portraiture of American slavery that is read by tens of thousands, causing many of them to weep and pray, and resolve that they will strive, while life shall last, for its overthrow and annihilation."[86]

William Lloyd Garrison wrote in the *Liberator* that when he read the novel, he was moved by it. He said that he expected the novel's effect would be "prodigious, and therefore eminently serviceable to the tremendous conflict now waged for the immediate and entire suppression of slavery on the American soil."[87]

Frederick Douglass wrote that Stowe's novel had "rekindled the slumbering embers of anti-slavery zeal into active flame. Its recitals have baptized with holy fire myriads who cared nothing for the bleeding slave."[88]

The Higher Law

Uncle Tom's Cabin is an entertaining story. Its characters are unforgettable. The famous scene of Eliza's desperate flight across the Ohio River to save her son and escape slavery is thrilling. Other than the Bible, it was the best-selling book of the nineteenth century. It was also a significant book. As stated by David Reynolds, author of *Mightier than the Sword: Uncle Tom's Cabin and the Battle for America*, "No book in American history molded public opinion more powerfully than *Uncle Tom's Cabin*."[89]

The novel describes the plight of enslaved people and fugitives in a family story to which white Americans could relate. Beyond that, Harriet brought passion to her writing. She was outraged because slave trading in the South divided families of enslaved people, separating children from their parents. She thought that she knew how enslaved mothers and fathers felt when their children were sold away from them in the slave trade because she had recently suffered painful loss when her eighteen-month-old son died of cholera. As she said, "It was at *his* dying bed and at *his* grave that I learnt what a poor slave mother may feel when her child is torn away from her."[90]

From the start, separations caused by slave trading drove her story. In the opening chapter, a Kentucky plantation owner who needs money to pay his debts negotiates the sale to a slave trader of Uncle Tom, who manages his farm, and a four- or five-year-old boy. Thus, the stage is set for the two main plots of *Uncle Tom's Cabin*. One is of escape, and the other is of bondage. In the so-called slave narratives of the time, men escaped while women remained in bondage, often taking care of children. Harriet, however, added a twist, making the escape stories feature women while that of bondage is Uncle Tom's.

Having overheard the conversation of the plantation owner and the slave trader, Eliza acts on what she has learned to save her child. She flees with the boy toward free states to the north. Slave catchers pursue. They continue even after she crosses the Ohio River on ice floes and makes it to the other side. With the help of whites, she and her son join her husband

Uncle Tom's Cabin presented the thrilling escape of Eliza with her son. Pursued by slave catchers, she fled toward the Ohio River. As they came near, she "vaulted sheer over the turbid current by the shore, on to the raft of ice beyond." The ice on which she landed "pitched and creaked as her weight came on it." But she moved on. "With wild cries and desperate energy she leaped to another and still another cake;—stumbling—leaping—slipping—and springing upwards again." Finally, she reached Ohio. *Poster, 1886 revival of* Uncle Tom's Cabin, *Library of Congress.*

and make it to Canada. The escape story specifically focuses on the Fugitive Slave Law. The heroes are the runaways and the whites who assist them. The villains are the slave catchers who enforce the law.

While Eliza and her family escape, Uncle Tom is sold to the slave trader, who sells him to the St. Clares. When the slave owner dies, his estate sells Uncle Tom to plantation owner Simon Legree. This story shows the cruelty of Simon Legree as a slave owner and of the laws that put Legree in a position to act so cruelly. This attacks the domestic slave trade. In 1808, Congress had abolished the foreign slave trade. As Harriet noted sarcastically, "Trading Negroes from Africa, dear reader, is so horrid! But trading them in Kentucky—that's quite another thing!"[91]

After Uncle Tom's bondage story, Harriet wrote how the enslaved Cassy convinces Legree that his house was haunted by playing on his superstitious mind. As a result of this ploy, she and Emmeline escape and return to their families.

Both the escape and the bondage plots affirm the Higher Law doctrine. As Stowe noted, regardless of what appears to be taking place on a plantation, "over and above the scene there broods a portentous shadow—the shadow of *law*."[92]

Stowe was the leading advocate of the Higher Law doctrine, an idea that her brothers Henry and Charles had supported. Even before writing *Uncle Tom's Cabin*, Harriet had written about the Higher Law. In August 1850, Bailey had published a story by her about the Fugitive Slave Law. In the story, called "The Freeman's Parable," a family of enslaved fugitives asks a farmer for food. Obeying the law against aiding fugitives from slavery, he refuses, after which the family is captured. In a dream, the farmer goes to heaven to face Jesus, who condemns him for failing to aid suffering people. Harriet explained the Higher Law point of the parable: "Of late, there seem to be many in this nation, who seem to think that there is no standard of right and wrong higher than an act of Congress, or an interpretation of the Constitution."[93]

Frederick Douglass wrote of *Uncle Tom's Cabin*, "We doubt if abler arguments have ever been presented in favor of the 'Higher Law' than may be found here [in] Mrs. Stowe's truly great work."[94]

THE NOVEL WAS TRUTHFUL

Supporters of slavery vigorously attacked *Uncle Tom's Cabin* and its author for misrepresenting the facts of the conditions of enslaved people. To express outrage, one southerner even mailed Stowe an ear cut from the head of an enslaved person, enclosing a handwritten note that this was the effect of her defense of "D—d niggers." They asserted that slavery was humane and that slave owners had an economic reason for treating the people they owned well. The book showed just the opposite: that well-meaning slave owners would break up families because they needed to pay debts and also that families of deceased slave owners sold people and divided families as part of settling estates.[95]

In response to these attacks, Stowe wrote a 259-page book that she said was based on a "mountain of materials." Some of the materials she had while writing *Uncle Tom's Cabin*, and some she obtained after the book was published.[96] While not as popular as the novel itself, *A Key to Uncle Tom's Cabin* was another bestseller; 40,000 copies of the book were ordered in advance of its publication. In the first year, 100,000 copies were sold.

176   KEY TO UNCLE TOM'S CABIN.

describing fugitive slaves. From these descriptions one may learn a vast many things. The author will here give an assortment of them, taken at random. It is a commentary on the contented state of the slave population that the writer finds two or three always, and often many more, in every one of the hundreds of Southern papers examined.

In reading the following little sketches of "slaves as they are," let the reader notice:

1. The color and complexion of the majority of them.

2. That it is customary either to describe slaves by some *scar*, or to say "*No scars recollected.*"

3. The *intelligence* of the parties advertised.

4. The number that *say they are free* that are to be *sold to pay jail-fees.*

Every one of these slaves has a history,—a history of woe and crime, degradation, endurance, and wrong. Let us open the chapter:

South-side Democrat, Oct. 28, 1852. Petersburgh, Virginia:

REWARD.

Twenty-five dollars, with the payment of all necessary expenses, will be given for the apprehension and delivery of my man CHARLES, if taken on the Appomattox river, or within the precincts of Petersburgh. He ran off about a week ago, and, if he leaves the neighborhood, will no doubt make for Farmville and Petersburgh. He is *a mulatto*, rather below the medium height and size, but well proportioned, and very active and sensible. He is aged about 27 years, has a mild, submissive look, *and will, no doubt, show the marks of a recent whipping, if taken.* He must be delivered to the care of Peebles, White, Davis & Co.

                       R. H. DeJarnett,
Oct. 25—3t.   Lunenburgh.

Poor Charles! — *mulatto!* — has a mild, submissive look, and will probably show marks of a recent whipping!

Kosciusko Chronicle, Nov. 24, 1852:

COMMITTED

To the Jail of Attila County, on the 8th instant, a negro boy, who calls his name GREEN, and says he belongs to James Gray, of Winston County. Said boy is about 20 years old, *yellow complexion*, round face, *has a scar on his face, one on his left thigh, and one in his left hand*, is about 5 feet 6 inches high. Had on when taken up a cotton check shirt, Linsey pants, new cloth cap, and was riding a large roan horse about 12 or 14 years old and thin in order. The owner is requested to come forward, prove property, pay charges, and take him away, or he will be sold to pay charges.

             E. B. Sanders, Jailer A. C.
Oct. 12, 1842.   n12tf.

Capitolian Vis-a-Vis, West Baton Rouge, Nov. 1, 1852:

$100 REWARD.

Runaway from the subscriber, in Randolph County, on the 18th of October, a *yellow* boy, named JIM. This boy is 19 years old, *a light mulatto with dirty sunburnt hair, inclined to be straight*; he is just 5 feet 7 inches high, and slightly made. He had on when he left a black cloth cap, black cloth pantaloons, a plaided sack coat, a fine shirt, and brogan shoes. One hundred dollars will be paid for the recovery of the above-described boy, if taken out of the State, or fifty dollars if taken in the State.

                   Mrs. S. P. Hall.
Nov. 4, 1852.   Huntsville, Mo.

American Baptist, Dec. 20, 1852:

TWENTY DOLLARS REWARD FOR A PREACHER.

The following paragraph, headed "Twenty Dollars Reward," appeared in a recent number of the *New Orleans Picayune*:

"Run away from the plantation of the undersigned the negro man Shedrick, a preacher, 5 feet 9 inches high, about 40 years old, but looking not over 23, *stamped N. E. on the breast, and having both small toes cut off.* He is of a very dark complexion, with eyes small but bright, *and a look quite insolent.* He dresses good, and was arrested as a runaway at Donaldsonville, some three years ago. The above reward will be paid for his arrest, by addressing Messrs. Armant Brothers, St. James parish, or A. Miltenberger & Co., 30 Carondelet-street."

Here is a preacher who is branded on the breast and has both toes cut off,—and *will* look insolent yet! There's depravity for you!

Jefferson Inquirer, Nov. 27, 1852:

$100 DOLLARS REWARD.

RANAWAY from my plantation, in Bolivar County, Miss., a negro man named MAY, aged 40 years, 5 feet 10 or 11 inches high, *copper colored*, and very straight; his front teeth are good and stand a little open; stout through the shoulders, *and has some scars on his back that show above the skin plain, caused by the whip;* he frequently hiccups when eating, if he has not got water handy; he was pursued into Ozark County, Mo., and there left. I will give the above reward for his confinement in jail, so that I can get him.

             James H. Cousar,
     Victoria, Bolivar County, Mississippi.
Nov. 13, 1m.

Delightful master to go back to, this man must be!

The Alabama Standard has for its motto:

"RESISTANCE TO TYRANTS IS OBEDIENCE TO GOD."

Date of Nov. 29th, this advertisement:

COMMITTED

To the Jail of Choctaw County, by Judge Young, of Marengo County, a RUNAWAY SLAVE, who

In *A Key to Uncle Tom's Cabin*, Mrs. Stowe used southern newspaper advertisements to describe how enslaved people were treated. On page 176, she said, "Every one of these slaves has a history—a history of woe and crime, degradation, endurance, and wrong." *Author's collection.*

This wood engraving of Theodore Dwight Weld was created in about 1885 as an illustration for a biography of William Lloyd Garrison. *Library of Congress.*

In Harriet's response, she used the approach and style of Theodore Dwight Weld's best-selling antislavery book of fifteen years before, *American Slavery as It Is: Testimony of a Thousand Witnesses*. She knew Weld when he was a student at Lane Theological Seminary and had attended the so-called Lane Debates that he led: eighteen days of prayer meetings, at the end of which the students almost unanimously voted for immediate abolition as opposed to colonization. When he was an agent of the American Anti-Slavery Society, Weld collected southern newspapers and selected articles and advertisements to describe slavery out of southerners' own words. Harriet quoted from Weld's book and expanded on it to include recent materials. Weld's wife, Angelina Grimke Weld, said that Stowe told her she "kept that book in her work basket by day, and slept with it under her pillow at night, till its facts crystalized into Uncle Tom."[97]

In *A Key to Uncle Tom's Cabin*, Harriet responded to several criticisms. Since questions had been raised about the characters in her novel, she described "the incidents by which different parts [of the story] were suggested." She pointed to a recent article from the *New York Courier and Enquirer* "as summing up, in a clear, concise and intelligible form, the principal objections" to her book. The article noted that the novel presented slavery "in three dark aspects," namely, the treatment of enslaved people, the separation of families and their lack of religious instruction. In response, she quoted southern statutes and case reports to describe what slavery was under southern laws. Her critics argued, for instance, that it was unrealistic for her to portray Simon Legree as having murdered his own slave. She responded by citing southern cases with facts that were more brutal than her description of Tom's murder. She concluded her presentation of southern law by arguing that slavery "is absolute despotism, of the most unmitigated form."[98]

Harriet described in detail the May 1852 interviews of Milly Edmonson and her daughters, Mary and Emily. In relating their experiences, Harriet explained the truth of her narrative of enslaved mothers in *Uncle Tom's Cabin*. The Edmonson family, like all those in slavery, had to live with the "express fact" that a mother's "service and value was to consist in breeding up her own children to be sold in the slave-market." In telling of the conditions of slave pens that Mary and Emily faced awaiting auction, she communicated the fears of being sold that enslaved people lived with daily.[99]

THEATRICAL PRODUCTIONS

The impact of *Uncle Tom's Cabin* resulted from readership that exceeded its sales by many times. In addition, multiple theatrical productions drew audiences of people who did not even know about the existence of the novel.

Almost immediately after the installments in the *National Era* were completed and the novel was published in book form, dramatizations of the novel appeared. Because of the copyright laws of the day, theatrical companies did not need to have permission to produce plays based on a novel, nor did they have to pay royalties. Harriet wrote a play in 1853 that was performed only a few times. But in 1853, two versions of the novel were competing with each other in New York City, one at the National Theatre and the other, produced by P.T. Barnum, at his American Museum on Broadway.

Theatrical productions of *Uncle Tom's Cabin* generated an enthusiastic response from working people. Among those who filled the theaters were b'hoys or rowdies like those who had broken into Lewis Tappan's house and burned his furnishings in 1834 and those who had prevented Wendell Phillips from delivering his speech at the American Anti-Slavery Society meeting in May 1850. Now they were cheering the fugitives and hissing the slave owners. The *New York Tribune* reported, "The b'hoys were on the side of the fugitives. The pro-slavery feeling had departed from among them…They believed in the higher law." William Lloyd Garrison wrote in the *Liberator*, "O, it was a sight worth seeing, those ragged, coatless men and boys in the

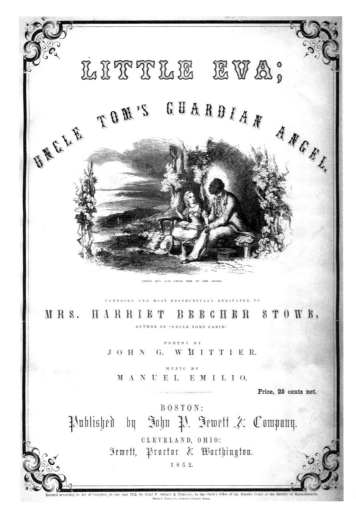

The cover of the 1852 sheet music of "Little Eva; Uncle Tom's Guardian Angel." The picture by Hammatt Billings is from the 1852 first edition of *Uncle Tom's Cabin*, showing Little Eva and Uncle Tom. He is dressed as a southern gentleman and appears as a father figure, leaning toward Eva. *Collection of Plymouth Church.*

pit (the very *material* of which mobs are made) cheering the strongest and sublimest anti-slavery sentiments! The whole audience was at times melted to tears, and I own I was no exception."[100]

Many of the plays included songs, just as Harriet had included the text of hymns in her novel. Minstrel shows were popular, and the advertising of *Uncle Tom's Cabin* theatrical productions communicated that there would be singing and dancing. In response to Stowe's novel, Stephen Foster wrote in the sketchbook he kept in the 1850s a song he called "Poor Uncle Tom, Good Night." The chorus of the song was:

Oh good night, good night, good night
Poor uncle Tom
Grieve not for your old Kentucky home
You'r bound for a better land
Old Uncle Tom

Foster did not publish the original song, although a later version, "My Old Kentucky Home," was often one of the songs used in *Uncle Tom's Cabin* plays. According to playbills in archives, the song was not sung by Uncle Tom but rather by either George Harris or Topsy.[101]

Merchandising tie-ins of all sorts undoubtedly increased the popularity of the novel and the plays. Called "Uncle Tomitudes," the various engravings and paintings on many media anticipated twentieth-century mass merchandising. They were representations of characters or scenes from the novel on a variety of items. They appeared in pictures on boxes, biscuit tins, mugs, jars, spoons, plates, jigsaw puzzles, chinaware, trinkets and playing cards, as well as in statues of figurine sets. Many items portrayed sympathetic depictions of enslaved people. Some showed slavery's cruel side. Since the tie-ins often included an antislavery message, they expanded the impact of *Uncle Tom's Cabin*.

THE NOVEL CHANGED ATTITUDES

In 1856, British professor Nassau William Senior published a pamphlet entitled *American Slavery*. He asserted that immediately after it was passed, the Fugitive Slave Law was popular with most people because of widespread racial prejudice. For the next two years, working people "enjoyed the excitement of a negro hunt as much as our rustics enjoy following a fox hunt." *Uncle Tom's Cabin*, he argued, changed that. During the play, when Eliza escaped with her son across the Ohio River, "the theatre rung and rung with applause." "Public sympathy," he concluded, "turned in favour of the slave."

Senior pointed out that the 1854 capture of Anthony Burns in Boston had required federal troops to march Burns to a ship through a crowd of fifty thousand people shouting, "Kidnapper! Slave Catcher! Shame! Shame!" He predicted that the government would not return another fugitive to slavery again. He concluded, "As far as the Northern States are concerned, Uncle

Tom has repealed the Fugitive Slave Law." South Carolina planter John Bell agreed that the plays had nullified the law.[102]

The actions of the New York State Vigilance Committee confirmed these opinions, for as Anthony Lane recalled, "At first, we sent [fugitives] to Canada, but after a while, sent them only to Syracuse, and the centre of the State."[103]

The purpose of the Compromise of 1850, with its Fugitive Slave Law, had been to put the slavery issue to rest and end sectional divisions that divided the country. Within a year or so after the various bills of the compromise had been enacted, it had seemed that most Americans had moved on and forgotten contentious issues, except for a small group of abolitionists that argued against the Fugitive Slave Law and kept the subject alive. Harriet Beecher Stowe and her *Uncle Tom's Cabin*, with its plays and tie-in merchandise, changed all that.

The remaining years of the 1850s would be different from the earlier years because of Harriet's book and its acceptance by the public. Responding to public opinion, changes in antislavery organizations and political parties occurred, and a law opening the Kansas Territory to settlement led to violence between southerners and northerners.

CHAPTER 5

THE CHURCH OF THE HOLY RIFLES

On October 24, 1854, Lewis Tappan wrote that the mission of the American and Foreign Anti-Slavery Society "is about ended." As to what that society had been doing recently, he said, "I frankly reply, very little." He explained that people in the northern states had been "awakening to the evils, encroachments and desperation of slavery," and therefore, the continuation of the "old" antislavery societies "seems needless." He said that "a vast change has taken place in public sentiment."

Since 1840, Tappan said, the society had accomplished much for the cause. It had "contributed essentially" to the "anti-slavery sentiment now extensively prevailing in the free States." It had established the antislavery newspaper, the *National Era*, which had published *Uncle Tom's Cabin* and "other influences greatly exceeding in magnitude the effect of all other anti-slavery papers in the country." It had sent out a "vast amount of anti-slavery intelligence" and published several "standard anti-slavery works."[104]

Some five months later, on April 4, 1855, Tappan and George Whipple with four other leaders of the antislavery society that was ending joined two friends from upstate New York, Frederick Douglass and Gerrit Smith, to issue a call for people to attend a convention of "Radical Political Abolitionists" to be held at Syracuse from June 26 to June 28, 1855. Commenting on the call, Tappan said that the founders of the antislavery society had previously thought that under the United States Constitution, they could not abolish slavery in the states "except by agreement and persuasion." Over time, however, they had concluded "something more could be done." Slaveholding

was "not only sinful but illegal and unconstitutional, and within the power of the people of the U.S. through the national legislature and judiciary." The purpose of the new abolition society was "to secure the immediate and unconditional abolition of American Slavery."[105]

Before the convention took place, the New York City Abolition Society was founded, with the purpose of abolishing slavery by means of "the Constitution *or otherwise.*" The word "otherwise" suggested that its activities would involve more than persuasion. Dr. James McCune Smith even underlined the words "or otherwise," explaining that he understood that they meant "fight." At the convention, he helped develop the party's platform, which affirmed violence as a means of ending slavery. McCune Smith served as convention chairman. For the first time in American

Top: Frederick Douglass. *Author's collection.*

Bottom: Dr. James McCune Smith. *Author's collection.*

This print of a photograph of John Brown was taken in the 1850s. *Library of Congress.*

history, a black man chaired a national political convention, a clear message that the party leadership included blacks. At the end of the three days, those attending unanimously passed a resolution thanking him for presiding with "ability, urbanity, and impartiality."[106]

The Radical Political Abolitionist organization, later called the American Abolition Society, was a combination of an antislavery society and a political party. It was as if the American and Foreign Anti-Slavery Society had joined together with the Liberty Party. In addition, the society published a monthly newspaper, the *Radical Abolitionist*, edited by William Goodell.

John Brown attended the convention on his way to join five of his sons in Kansas. On the third day of the meeting, Gerrit Smith read to the convention two letters from Brown's sons. The letters described "hundreds and thousands of the meanest and most desperate of men, armed to the teeth with Revolvers, Bowie Knives, Rifles and Cannon." They were organized and paid by slaveholders. Against them were antislavery men who were not well armed or organized. Brown's sons asked for weapons to defend themselves. When Smith had finished reading the letters, Brown appealed for money and arms to take with him to Kansas. Lewis Tappan was the only one at the convention to oppose violent means. Most agreed that help was necessary, and Frederick Douglass encouraged people to make contributions. Brown received money and some weapons to take with him.[107]

Repealing the Missouri Compromise

Public opinion supported settlement of the frontier and connecting the Midwest with California by a transcontinental railroad. In January 1854, Illinois senator Stephen A. Douglas introduced a bill to organize the Kansas and Nebraska territories west of the slave state of Missouri. He included a provision that southerners insisted on noting that the 1820 Missouri Compromise ban on slavery in the Louisiana Purchase north of latitude thirty-six degrees, thirty minutes, was "inoperative and void." The bill provided that the decision on whether slavery would be allowed or banned in the territory would be made by the settlers themselves, an approach known as "popular sovereignty."

By proposing to repeal the compromise that had been the understanding between northerners and southerners for a generation, Senator Douglas unleashed a storm of outrage from those in the Plymouth Church community and elsewhere in the North. Immediately after Douglas introduced his bill, Harriet Beecher Stowe helped organize a rally against the bill in Boston, bringing her brother Henry together with William Lloyd Garrison and Wendell Phillips. She

wrote an "Appeal" urging women to pray and to petition Congress to stop the bill. She also organized signing petitions. The editors of the *Independent* wrote articles opposing the bill. Henry Ward Beecher opposed the bill in sermons, lectures and articles in the *Independent*.[108] Despite strong opposition, however, the bill passed and was signed by President Franklin Pierce on May 30, 1854.

This daguerreotype of Senator Stephen A. Douglas of Illinois was taken by Mathew Brady. *Library of Congress.*

Popular sovereignty caused proslavery and Free-Soil factions to enter a competition over slavery in Kansas. In the November 1854 election of a territorial delegate to Congress and in the March 1855 election of a territorial legislature, Missouri "border ruffians" crossed into Kansas to vote for the proslavery candidates. In both elections, the proslavery candidates won handily. At that time, the proslavery candidates probably would have won a fair election, but a later Congressional Committee concluded that they had won with many "fraudulent" ballots.

By the fall of 1855, the Free-Soil residents of Kansas outnumbered those who were proslavery. They decided to elect a territorial government of their own. They called a convention to draw up a free-state constitution and held elections for delegates. Thus, by January 1856, Kansas had two territorial governments: a proslavery "official" one in Lecompton, elected fraudulently, and a Free-Soil "unofficial" one in Topeka that had used popular sovereignty to establish its government.

"Beecher's Bibles" in "Bleeding Kansas"

In response to southerners being "armed to the teeth" as John Brown's sons reported, Free-Soil settlers armed themselves. The New England Emigrant Aid Society, established in the summer of 1854 to promote Free-Soil settlement of Kansas, sent an agent to Kansas to represent them there. Three days after the election of the proslavery territorial legislature, the agent sent an urgent request to Boston for two hundred Sharps breech-loading rifles and two cannons.[109]

Even before the Free-Soil settlers had elected their own legislature, violence had erupted in Kansas. On November 21, 1855, the killing of a proslavery man triggered other violent acts. On December 1, some 1,500 Missourians crossed the border and into the Wakarusa Valley to lay siege to Lawrence in what was called the "Wakarusa War." Before this could become more than a skirmish, the territorial governor went to Lawrence and persuaded both sides to disband. A severe winter prevented continued violence at that time.

In February 1856, Beecher preached a sermon entitled "Defence of Kansas" that was later published in the *Independent* and also as a pamphlet. In it, he likened antislavery forces in Kansas to freedom fighters, drawing a parallel between the war in "Bleeding Kansas" and the American

The so-called Beecher's Bibles rifles were Model 1853 single-shot breech-loading carbines, designed by Christian Sharps. Able to be fired at the rate of eight to ten rounds per minute, the rifle used a paper cartridge and shot a .52-caliber bullet from a barrel that was twenty-one and a half inches long. The weapon, known for its accuracy and long range, had an effective range of five hundred yards. Based on its serial number, this rifle was with John Brown at Harper's Ferry in 1859. *National Firearms Museum, nramuseum.com.*

The "Beecher Bible and Rifle Church" was established in June 1857. The church building was completed in 1862. This photograph shows the church building as it exists today. It continues to hold Sunday worship services. *Collection of Plymouth Church.*

Revolutionary War. He argued that people had to be prepared to defend freedom and appealed for money and arms.[110]

That same month, Beecher said that he "believed that the Sharps rifle was a truly moral agency, and that there was more moral power in one of those instruments, so far as the slaveholders of Kansas were concerned, than in a hundred Bibles." Beecher continued, saying, "You might just as well…read the Bible to Buffaloes" as to the Missouri slaveholders who were fighting in Kansas, "but they have a supreme respect for the logic that is embodied in Sharps rifle."[111]

In March 1856, Beecher attended a meeting at North Congregational Church in New Haven to raise money for men of the Connecticut Kansas Colony who were going to Kansas as settlers. He made a stirring speech to the men. When he finished, an announcement was made that the men going to Kansas were prepared to farm but were not armed to fight. A Yale professor pledged to pay twenty-five dollars to purchase a Sharps rifle. Beecher announced that if funds for twenty-five rifles could be raised that night, he would pledge to match that with twenty-five more from Plymouth Church. A man named Mr. Killam made the next pledge. "Killam," Beecher joked, "that's a significant name in connection with a Sharps rifle." That evening, those at the meeting made pledges for twenty-seven rifles. In September 1856, the *Brooklyn Daily Eagle* referred to Beecher as "the Rev. Killem Beecher."[112]

Shortly after the meeting at North Church, men heading to Kansas calling themselves the "Beecher Bible and Rifle Colony" marched through New Haven. Each carried a Sharps rifle and a Bible from Plymouth Church with the motto, "Be ye steadfast and unmovable." The Beecher Bible and Rifle Colony built a church in Wabaunsee, Kansas, called the "Beecher Bible and Rifle Church."[113]

Later, the Plymouth Church congregation raised money for another twenty-five rifles that were sent to Kansas, accompanied by twenty-five Bibles. In shipping weapons to Kansas through the slave state of Missouri, wooden boxes were labeled as containing such innocuous items as "crockery" or "tools." Plymouth Church shipped Sharps rifles to Kansas in boxes marked "Bibles." The press picked up on this and called Sharps rifles in the hands of Free-Soil settlers in Kansas "Beecher's Bibles," and Plymouth Church became known as the "Church of the Holy Rifles."[114]

Being a noted abolitionist church and urging the use of rifles (and, therefore, violence) could be dangerous. In June 1856, Sunday newspapers reported that a "gang of roughs" from New York City intended to come to Brooklyn for the purpose of "cleaning out the d----d abolition nest at Plymouth Church" and dispensing with the services of Beecher. Those in the congregation prepared to defend themselves. Brooklyn officials were notified, and armed plainclothes police attended worship. Gang members were identified. During worship, an object was thrown through a window, breaking it, and a bullet was found on a windowsill, but nothing else occurred. At the end of the service, gang members were heard muttering curses about "abolitionists and nigger-worshippers." Otherwise, they left without violence.[115]

Beecher's attacks against slavery drew opposition. Some argued that a minister should confine his speaking to the Bible and purely religious subjects. Indeed, a banner carried in an 1856 procession read, "Henry Ward Beecher had better stick to the pulpit." Beecher thought otherwise.

Beecher and Plymouth Church were not to be deterred and continued to be active in helping individual black people find freedom. After worship on June 1, 1856, Beecher announced that a slave trader in Richmond had bought a girl from her master, pitied her fate and decided to set her free. He had paid money but needed $500 to purchase her freedom. At this point, Beecher called Sarah and asked his congregation, "What shall you do now? May she read her liberty in your eyes? Shall she go free?" More than $700 was raised, not including jewelry. Lewis Tappan's pledge to make up the difference was not necessary.[116] At many worship services, Beecher announced that a black person would be standing near the door asking for money to purchase his or her family out of slavery.

The spring of 1856 brought more violence to Kansas. Proslavery Judge Samuel Lecompte instructed a grand jury to indict three members of the free-state government for treason. Missourians were deputized as a posse to attack Lawrence, where those indicted lived. Thus, on May 21, after they discovered that those indicted had departed, about eight hundred Missourians threw two printing presses in the river, burned the hotel and another building and looted the town. Free-Soil spokesmen called this the "Sack of Lawrence."

Throughout the summer and early fall of 1856, various groups of armed men marched across Kansas, terrorizing settlers and killing enough people to justify the term "Bleeding Kansas." In addition to newspapers in Kansas—such as the *Herald of Freedom*, which had wide circulation in New England—New York and Washington newspapers had correspondents in Kansas. John H. Kagi of the *National Era* was one of the best antislavery reporters. While some recent historians have argued that contemporary reporters exaggerated the fighting in Kansas, Nicole Etcheson described

Henry Ward Beecher's freedom auction of "Sarah" at Plymouth Church in June 1856. Her last name was either Churchman or Sheffer. *Collection of Plymouth Church.*

the violence of "bleeding Kansas."[117] In 1856, when a new territorial governor arrived, he put an end to the violence for the time being.

A SIGNIFICANT NEW HYMNAL

From the start of his ministry at Plymouth Church, Henry Ward Beecher encouraged singing by the congregation as a means of creating community. At Plymouth and in many churches, the congregation had only the words without the music. To help congregational singing, Beecher wanted to have a hymnal with both words and music on the same page. He concluded that the only solution was for Plymouth to publish its own hymnal.

A first attempt did not satisfy him. Then, in 1851, Henry's brother, Charles, was called as

Above: *The Plymouth Collection of Hymns and Tunes* was the first American hymnal to have the words and music on the same page. It was also notable for its antislavery hymns such as John Newton's "Amazing Grace." *Author's collection.*

Opposite, bottom: Reverend Charles Beecher. This image is taken from the Beecher family daguerreotype by Mathew Brady Studios in about 1859. *Harriet Beecher Stowe Center, Hartford, Connecticut.*

minister of a church in Newark. Since Charles had been his music director in Indiana, Henry had a familiar collaborator. Also, Plymouth's new organist, John Zundel, worked on the project. In addition, Susan Raymond Howard is reported to have worked on the hymnal.[118] The work that they completed in 1855 was entitled *Plymouth Collection of Hymns and Tunes*.

In *Uncle Tom's Cabin*, Harriet Beecher Stowe included verses of a dozen hymns sung by Uncle Tom and other enslaved characters in her novel. Possibly as a result of Harriet and the influence of her novel, the *Plymouth Collection* had a selection of antislavery hymns under index subjects including "emancipation," "equality," "freedom," "slaves" and "slavery." The book also contained thirty-four hymns written by John Newton, author of the text for "Amazing Grace," a hymn that Uncle Tom sang after having been beaten by Simon Legree. The book contained eleven hymns that had been written by abolitionist poet John Greenleaf Whittier, a founding member of the American Anti-Slavery Society. It also included three hymns written by Harriet Beecher Stowe.

REALIGNMENT OF POLITICAL PARTIES

Until this time, major political parties had always been national, seeking votes in both the North and the South, which meant that they had to have platforms that appealed to both the sections. The Whig Party split between northerners and southerners over disputes about slavery, lost the 1852 presidential election in a landslide and disintegrated. Groups calling themselves "Republicans" formed with the single principle of opposition to expansion of slavery beyond the existing slave states. They were amazingly successful. In the year they organized, these Republicans gained control of the House of Representatives. The emergence of a major political party appealing only to northerners and seeking to restrict slavery in the federal territories changed the political landscape.

In 1856, Republicans nominated as presidential candidate John C. Frémont, nicknamed "the Pathfinder," from California. Beecher helped the *New York Times* publisher Henry J. Raymond draft for Frémont his "Address to the American People" at the Republican convention.[119]

Tasker Howard had come to know Frémont during trips he had made to San Francisco in connection with his shipping business. When Frémont was nominated, Howard contributed use of his New York office to become headquarters for the campaign. He also introduced Beecher to Frémont. Beecher took a leave of absence from Plymouth Church to campaign for Frémont. Under the banner of "Free Soil, Free Speech, Free Men, Fremont," the campaign framed the issue of the extension of slavery in the territories. Beecher made "Bleeding Kansas" a prime issue in the campaign. In addition, Beecher defended Frémont when he was accused of being a "papist" because his father had been a Catholic and he and his wife had been married in a ceremony officiated by a Catholic priest. Beecher asserted that Frémont was "as good a Protestant as John Knox." The *Independent* also supported the Republican presidential candidate.[120]

In 1856, the Radical Abolitionists nominated Gerrit Smith for president on a platform calling for abolition of slavery in the states. Smith never had a chance. He received only 165 votes in his home state of New York. The party had not expected him to win but had nominated him to communicate their principles to the public.

As a part of his campaign, Democratic candidate James Buchanan warned that a Frémont victory would lead to civil war. Buchanan won the election, polling almost 58 percent of the vote. Frémont's name was not on the ballot in thirteen slaveholding states. However, the Electoral College results indicated that if the Republicans could win two more states, Pennsylvania and Illinois, they would win in 1860.

Both of the issues of the 1856 election, the Democrats' idea of popular sovereignty and the Republican Party's platform to limit slavery to the existing slaveholding states, were based on the power under the Constitution to control slavery. At that time, the Supreme Court had before it a case that might change the legal context in the 1860 campaign.

CHAPTER 6

CHALLENGES IN CRISIS YEARS

In March 1857, two days after President Buchanan's inauguration, the Supreme Court delivered its *Dred Scott* decision.[121] In it, Chief Justice Roger Taney wrote the majority opinion for five southern and two northern justices who sought to resolve the national political controversy over the future of slavery.

The chief justice first decided that Scott did not have the right to sue in United States courts because he was not a citizen. He asserted that blacks were not among the people who made the Constitution and that they were not included among "all men" in the Declaration of Independence statement that "all men are created equal." At the time the Constitution was adopted, Taney stated, blacks had been regarded as "inferior beings" for more than a century, "so inferior that they had no rights which a white man was bound to respect."[122]

Taney then decided that when Scott lived for two years in Illinois and for two years in Fort Snelling within the Louisiana Purchase, he did not become free. He also decided that the Missouri Compromise was unconstitutional because Congress did not have power under the Constitution to restrict slavery in the territories. He asserted that the power that Congress had under the Constitution to "make all needful rules and regulations" in the territories was not relevant because rules and regulations were not laws. By so deciding, the chief justice overturned a major plank in the 1856 Republican platform that the Constitution conferred on Congress powers over the territories and that "in exercise of this power," Congress had "both the right and the imperative duty" to "prohibit" slavery in the territories.[123]

This engraving shows Chief Justice Roger B. Taney in the 1850s. *Library of Congress.*

Southerners claimed victory and asserted that the decision ended the slavery issue. The case did not, however, end agitation. Republicans said that the dissents of Associate Justices Benjamin Curtis and John McLean stated the law correctly. They strongly criticized the use of law and history in the majority decision. Justice Curtis presented evidence, contrary to Taney's opinion, that blacks were citizens in many states at the time of the adoption of the Constitution. Republican state legislatures passed resolutions stating that the decision was "not binding in law and conscience."[124]

The *Independent* attacked the decision as "the moral assassination of a race" and said that it "cannot be obeyed." The *Radical Abolitionist* noted that the Supreme Court had decided that the political issue of the limitation of slavery had become "obsolete." The paper asked antislavery advocates to rally to the issue of abolition, which, it said, was "the only issue that is worth anything, or that has vitality and significance enough, to rouse the energies of a free people."[125]

The 1858 Lincoln-Douglas debates on slavery demonstrated that the slavery issue had not been put to rest. Abraham Lincoln predicted that "another Supreme Court decision" might declare that the Constitution "does not permit a state to exclude slavery from its limits." Since the *Lemmon* case that Louis Napoleon brought (with the help of the New York State Vigilance Committee) was based on New York statutes excluding slavery from the state, this issue was very real for New Yorkers. Judge Paine's 1852 decision was affirmed by the New York State Supreme Court in 1857 and by the New York Court of Appeals in 1860. Since counsel retained by the State of Virginia argued the case before the latter court, it was anticipated that Virginia would take the case to the United States Supreme Court. By then, the committee and James Pennington had arranged for those freed in the *Lemmon* case to go to Canada.[126]

In December 1857, Lewis Tappan and Theodore Tilton applied to the Brooklyn City Court for a writ of habeas corpus for the release of a black fugitive who had "smuggled himself" aboard a ship from Savannah, Georgia, and arrived in New York. The ship captain had discovered the fugitive when they were at sea and, when the ship arrived at port, had him locked up in a house at Red Hook Point in Brooklyn under guard so he could be returned to his master. Probably applying the precedent of the *Lemmon* case that had been affirmed by the state Supreme Court earlier that year, the judge granted a writ of habeas corpus. The *Brooklyn Daily Eagle* speculated, "The fugitive is probably by this time recuperating his energies in the invigorating climate of Canada, and his detainers here are under bonds to answer on charges of misdemeanor and felony."[127]

An investigation of a new election of the Kansas legislature showed that, in two remote districts, 2,900 ballots were cast, although there were only 130 legal voters. In one district, 1,600 names had been copied into the rolls from an old Cincinnati city directory.

Meanwhile, the proslavery convention at Lecompton prepared a constitution. President Buchanan accepted it, saying that if he did not, southern states would secede. On February 2, 1858, he sent the Lecompton constitution to Congress with a recommendation that Kansas be admitted as a slave state. He said that the Supreme Court had determined in the *Dred Scott* case that "slavery exists in Kansas by virtue of the Constitution" and added, "Kansas is therefore at this moment as much a slave State as Georgia or South Carolina."[128]

With this, Senator Douglas confronted President Buchanan in an event that led to the Democratic Party being divided in the 1860 presidential election. Douglas argued that the Lecompton constitution was the result of "trickery" and made a mockery of popular sovereignty. He told the president that he would oppose it in Congress. The Senate approved admission, but the House, with northern Democrats joining the Republicans, defeated it. The Buchanan administration arranged another referendum on the Lecompton constitution. Free-Soil Kansans rejected it by more than six to one.

At about that time, violence returned to Kansas. In May 1858, a proslavery group abducted nine Free-Soil settlers from their cabins and shot them by firing squad. Five were killed. John Brown also came back. His band killed a slaveholder, freed eleven slaves, stole horses and took them to Canada.

In 1859, Free-Soil Kansans organized a Republican Party and elected two-thirds of the delegates to a new constitutional convention. In 1858 and 1859, respectively, Minnesota and Oregon were admitted as free states. When Kansas was admitted as a free state in January 1861, free states outnumbered slave states by four, and the South had lost parity in the Senate to block legislation adversely affecting slavery.

THE 1858 "BUSINESSMAN'S REVIVAL"

After the opening of the new meetinghouse on the first Sunday in January 1850, attendance at Sunday worship at Plymouth Church grew to overflowing. Many people came from New York City on ferryboats. When they asked how to find the church, they were told to "follow the crowds."[129]

The number of people who joined the membership of Plymouth Church also grew. Over the years from 1850 to 1857, 66 people on average were added to the membership each year. By January 1858, Plymouth Church had 863 members.[130]

A worldwide financial panic in 1857 led to a nationwide religious revival that continued through 1858. The panic started on August 11, 1857. On September 23, a missionary at a church in Manhattan opened a room for noontime prayer for businessmen. As numbers grew, he opened additional rooms. Similar prayer meetings were held in other churches and spread to other cities in upstate New York and New England. This revival was unique for its noon-hour interdenominational prayer meetings attended by businessmen. Because of this, it was called the "Businessman's Revival."

The revival commenced at Plymouth Church in early 1858. At first, Beecher did not attend. On March 11, he started to attend the morning prayer meetings and then attended daily. He also spoke to audiences in other churches and contributed a series of articles on revivalism to the *Independent*. The morning prayer meetings at Plymouth Church continued every day through July 3 and frequently thereafter.[131]

Folding chairs attached to the end of pews in the aisle were used to increase the seating capacity of the Plymouth Church meetinghouse. *Author's collection.*

At communion services in May and June, 442 people joined Plymouth Church that year, 369 of them by confession of faith and 73 by transfer from another church. Harriet Beecher Stowe and her son, Frederick, became Plymouth Church members in May.

Before the revival, strangers at worship services were seated on chairs and stools. After some experimentation during the revival, a church member invented and patented a simple folding chair design. The chairs were attached to the ends of pews in the aisles, increasing the seating capacity of the meetinghouse from 2,050 by some 500.[132]

The revival had results other than adding to church membership. It brought about cooperation among religious sects. It also helped intensify the religious fervor underlying antislavery sentiment and thereby prepared the North emotionally for the Civil War.

Probably as a result of the "high" achieved during the revival, the members of Plymouth Church and its minister came to believe in September 1858 that if the church building were twice its size, people would fill most, if not all, of the pews. Over the next two and a half years, the congregation made plans for the new building, purchased fourteen lots from Montague to Remsen Streets west of Hicks Street, obtained bids to build the structure and sought money to pay for it. During the next two years, only 36 members were added in 1859

View of Remsen Street in Brooklyn Heights in 1860s, looking west from Clinton Street. Shown on the right corner of the next block is the steeple of the Church of the Pilgrims. The proposed new Plymouth Church meetinghouse was to be located one block beyond the Church of the Pilgrims, between Remsen and Montague Streets. *Author's collection.*

and 43 in 1860, bringing the total membership to 1,320. At the annual meeting in January 1861, the trustees decided to abandon the project. A Plymouth Church historian described the proposed new church project as a "fiasco."[133]

JOHN BROWN SOUGHT TO FREE SLAVES

On October 16, 1859, after seeking to solicit funds from friends and acquaintances—including Lewis Tappan, who refused to give him money—John Brown led thirteen whites and five blacks in an attack on the federal arsenal at Harpers Ferry, Virginia (now West Virginia). His purpose was to establish a stronghold to which enslaved people could flee and from which insurrections could be organized. He captured the arsenal without much resistance. On the next day, Brown and his men were surrounded by Virginia militia and, on the following day, assaulted by a company of U.S. marines. Ten of Brown's men were killed, and Brown was wounded. He was captured and charged with treason.

The news of Brown's attack was greeted in the South with fear of slave insurrections. The *Independent* called the attack the act of "a demented man." The paper admired his motives but did not condone his violence. It noted, "Misguided as he was by the zeal of the oppressed…in his motives, his spirit and his intentions, the bravest, truest, noblest man Virginia has seen since her revolutionary heroes passed away."[134]

In his October 30, 1859 sermon, Beecher pictured Brown as being a victim of the wrong in Kansas. He criticized the federal government for having failed to support the Free-Soilers in Kansas: "The United States Government had no marines for this occasion!" He identified John Brown as a potential American hero: "Let no man pray that Brown be spared. Let Virginia make him a martyr." He then criticized northerners for their poor treatment of blacks. He challenged northerners to set an example of how blacks should be treated and urged them to give freed slaves education and employment opportunities. During a speech about Brown at the Broadway Tabernacle, Beecher stamped on chains that he said had manacled Brown.[135]

Over the month following his capture, Brown became a folk hero. Brown's simple dignity and apparent sincerity during the trial and the days before his execution by hanging on December 2, 1859, led many in the North to regard him as a martyr. Within a little more than a year, Brown was indeed considered a martyr in the North, and "John Brown's Body Lies a-Mouldering in the Grave" became a U.S. Army marching song.

DEBATE OVER SUPPORT FOR MISSIONARIES

At the annual meeting of the church commencing on December 30, 1859, Lewis Tappan proposed a resolution for Plymouth Church to withhold its contributions to the American Board of Commissioners for Foreign Missions, which Lyman Beecher had helped found in 1810, and to give the money to the American Missionary Association, which Tappan had helped found as an antislavery missionary society. The board, in addition to its overseas activities, carried out mission work among the Choctaw and Cherokee tribes

This photograph is a copy of a carte de visite of Theodore Tilton, probably taken in the 1860s. *Collection of Plymouth Church.*

in Indian Territory. Some of these Indians had adopted the southern practice of owning enslaved people, and the Choctaw nation had passed laws supporting slavery. Some of the missionaries used enslaved people as servants. In the past, Tappan had asserted that the board should be investigated and exposed as the board condoned slavery and polygamy.[136] The board had taken an antislavery position but gave its missionaries discretion to implement the policy.

Debate on the resolution continued for five evenings in January 1860. Beecher supported the work of the board, asserting that he believed that the Indians would keep their promise to free the enslaved people that they held.

Near the end of the meetings, Theodore Tilton of the *Independent* newspaper made an impassioned speech. Born in New York City, Tilton had been educated at the Free Academy, now the College of the City of New York. Even though he was not a minister, his first assignment at the paper was as a reporter for the "Religious Intelligence" column. Having joined Plymouth Church in 1853, he had developed a friendship with Henry Bowen and Beecher, but his responsibility at the *Independent* increased as a result of his journalistic talent. During his speech, he accused Beecher of changing his position on slavery when he said that he was willing to admit slaveholders to the church. Tilton ended his argument by brandishing a rifle, dramatically revealing that this weapon was one of the rifles sent by Plymouth Church to Kansas and that it had been carried by none other than John Brown.

Beecher concluded by saying that he "would stay in the Church, and in the Union, and in the Board to get them in the right path and keep them there." On January 25, 1860, the congregation voted with Beecher to continue to make contributions to the board and also to support the American Missionary Association.[137]

Left: Ellen Mitchell. Annotated on the back of the photograph is the note, "1859, Plymouth Church paid $10,000 for her and her seven children, came from Richmond, VA." *Collection of Plymouth Church.*

Below: On the day after her baptism, Beecher took Rose to New York City and commissioned Eastman Johnson to paint her portrait. Johnson's work shows Rose with her "Freedom Ring." Johnson established a studio in New York in 1859. He made his reputation with an exhibition that featured his painting *Negro Life at the South*, popularly known as *Old Kentucky Home*. He was cofounder of the Metropolitan Museum of Art in New York City. *Hallmark Art Collection, Kansas City, Missouri.*

Plymouth Church continued to have "freedom auctions" and purchase the freedom of enslaved people. The church's treasurer's reports recorded purchases of freedom of seven people or groups of people between 1854 and 1860. The treasurer also noted that some funds for benevolent purposes did not pass through his hands. Thus, while he reported that he had paid less than $500 for the freedom of Ellen Mitchell and her children, a message on the back of a photograph in 1859 noted that the church paid $10,000 to free Ellen Mitchell and her seven children.[138]

On February 5, 1860, at the end of the worship service, Henry Ward Beecher called a nine-year-old enslaved girl named "Pinky" to the stage and told the congregation her story. Pinky's owner in Washington, D.C., planned to sell her to the Deep South, but he would allow her to be purchased for the price of $900. The congregation was so moved by the story that, when the collection plates were passed, $1,100 in money and jewelry had been collected.

Subsequently, Beecher baptized Pinky and gave her the name "Rose Ward." Rose was for Rose Terry, a poet who had put her ring in the plate, and Ward was his own middle name. He put the ring on Pinky's finger and told her "with this ring, I wed you to freedom."

ABRAHAM LINCOLN INVITED TO SPEAK AT PLYMOUTH CHURCH

In October 1859, a committee arranging an eight-lecture series invited Abraham Lincoln to speak at Plymouth Church. That committee included the publisher of the *Independent*, Joseph Richards, and Henry Bowen's nephew. When they asked Bowen about a speaker for the series, he recommended Lincoln as a person who would draw a crowd and make the lecture a success. The Young Men's Republican Union of New York City, fearing that few people would cross the icy East River, arranged to move the location of the speech to Cooper Institute in Manhattan.

On February 25, 1860, Lincoln arrived in New York and went to Henry Bowen's office at the *Independent*, where he learned that the site of the speech had been changed from a church to a political venue. On the next day, he joined Bowen in his pew for Sunday worship at Plymouth Church. He turned down an invitation for dinner, saying that he had to work on his speech to be given on the following day. On February 27, he walked up Broadway and

On the morning of his address, Abraham Lincoln had his portrait taken at Mathew Brady's Tenth Street gallery. Instead of taking his usual close-up head shot, Brady chose to emphasize Lincoln's height. He moved his camera away and had Lincoln stand while he took a three-quarters picture. He placed a pillar behind Lincoln's right shoulder and a pile of books on a table to his left. Because it would be a time exposure, Brady braced the back of Lincoln's head against an iron clamp to hold his head motionless, resulting in Lincoln's determined look. *Library of Congress.*

had his portrait taken at Mathew Brady's studio.

That evening, Lincoln delivered his address at Cooper Institute on the subject of the Republican position on slavery after the *Dred Scott* decision. He demonstrated that the Supreme Court had been wrong to declare that the Missouri Compromise was unconstitutional, as the Founding Fathers had spoken and acted in such a way that it was impossible to show that the Constitution "forbade the Federal Government to control as to slavery in the federal territories." He ended his address with the words, "Let us have faith that right makes might, and in that faith, let us dare to do our duty as we understand it." In this speech, Lincoln provided Republicans and abolitionists a basis for staying the course. The speech was printed in its entirety in newspapers in New York and elsewhere.[139]

After delivering the speech, Lincoln traveled in New England, visiting with his son at Phillips Exeter Academy in New Hampshire and giving speeches. After the two-week trip, he returned to Plymouth Church for Sunday worship on March 11, 1860. Something he had heard at the first service caused Lincoln to want to hear Beecher again.

When Lincoln was invited to speak at Plymouth Church, he was little known east of the Appalachian Mountains. The speech he gave at Cooper Institute changed that. Two months and twenty-one days after he gave the address, he was nominated as the Republican presidential candidate. When he met Mathew Brady a few months later, Lincoln said, "Brady and the Cooper Institute made me President." In his campaign for the nomination

CHALLENGES IN CRISIS YEARS

and for the presidency, the Cooper Institute address was the only speech he gave, and the Brady photograph was the only one his campaign used.[140]

Just as the Whig Party had split over slavery following the Kansas and Nebraska Act in 1854, the Democratic Party split over southern insistence that the slaveholders' constitution be accepted in Kansas. Thus, northern Democrats nominated Senator Stephen Douglas, while southern Democrats nominated the sitting vice president John C. Breckinridge of Kentucky. In addition, the remnant of the Whig Party in the South nominated John Bell of Tennessee.

Abolitionists were in a dilemma about the 1860 presidential campaign. For the first time, a political party with a platform that supported an antislavery position had a chance to win. But they also realized that the Republicans would not abolish slavery; they would only try to restrict slavery to existing states, even though the Supreme Court had said that was not possible. The party platform noted that "the new dogma" from the *Dred Scott* case that the Constitution "of its own force carries slavery into any or all of the territories" is "a dangerous political heresy." Another plank noted that "the normal condition of the territory of the United States is that of freedom" and that the party denied the authority of Congress to "give legal existence to slavery" in any federal territory.[141]

The Radical Abolitionist Party again nominated Gerrit Smith for president. Lewis Tappan debated whether to vote for Lincoln and finally decided to vote for Smith. Theodore Tilton, vice-president of the New York City Anti-Slavery Society, voted for Lincoln because a Republican victory would be a step in the right direction. During the presidential campaign, Beecher campaigned for Lincoln.

As New Yorkers were voting for president and other candidates, they were also voting on a proposal to abolish the $250 property qualification for black voters and to admit them to the polls on equal terms with whites. Frederick Douglass campaigned throughout upstate New York for this issue, which had been passed by the Republican legislature. Lincoln carried New York State by fifty thousand votes, but the suffrage proposal was defeated by a two-to-one margin.[142]

Lincoln won with 180 electoral votes, more than the 152 needed. He won all northern states. He was not listed on the ballot in ten slave states. He received just under 40 percent of the popular vote. Joshua Leavitt thought that Lincoln's election was the victorious end of the battle begun by the Liberty Party in 1840. "Thank God! Lincoln is chosen!" he cheered. "It is a joy to have lived to this day."[143]

On December 20, 1860, South Carolina seceded. Before Lincoln was inaugurated in March 1861, six other states had seceded as well.

CHAPTER 7

THE MISSION CHANGES IN WAR

By the time President Lincoln was inaugurated on March 4, seven Southern states had seceded, and four states seceded thereafter. When states seceded, Southern creditors refused to pay their debts, estimated to be $150 million ($4.2 billion in 2012 dollars). As a result, New York merchants who had extended credit to Southerners were forced into bankruptcy. Anticipating this, some New York merchants had refused to give credit to Southern customers in the fall of 1860. In 1861, Henry Bowen's store went bankrupt. He turned the *Independent* over to trustees, including his father-in-law, Lewis Tappan, who had managed and edited many papers. After dealing with his finances and bankruptcy, Bowen assumed ownership again. In 1862, President Lincoln appointed Bowen tax collector of the Third New York District, which included most of Brooklyn.[144]

When Southern states seceded, William Lloyd Garrison and Wendell Phillips of Boston-based American Anti-Slavery Society urged the United States to let the South go, although they changed their opinion when the war began. The American Missionary Association, led by Lewis Tappan and George Whipple, foresaw the possibility of emancipation as a result of the war. The association said that the war would open "one of the grandest fields for missionary labor" the world had ever known.[145]

On April 13, 1861, Confederates started the war by bombarding Fort Sumter, causing United States troops to surrender. Two days later, President Lincoln called for state militiamen to enter Federal service for three months under existing law. By Executive Order on May 3, he issued a call for three-year volunteers and increased the size of the regular army and navy. He also requested Congress to authorize three-year volunteers. To the start of the war and the raising of troops, Henry Ward Beecher brought the same enthusiasm that he had exhibited in raising funds and sending Sharps rifles to Free-Soil settlers in Kansas.

PLYMOUTH CHURCH EQUIPS THREE REGIMENTS

When President Lincoln issued his call for three-month volunteers, the Thirteenth Brooklyn Militia Regiment unanimously offered its services. Henry Ward Beecher was the regimental chaplain. Company G was known as the "Beecher Company." Plymouth Church members immediately raised money for the troops to purchase clothing at Brooks Brothers and elsewhere, as well as pistols and other equipment.[146]

On April 23, 1861, the regiment left the armory at Cranberry Street near Henry Street, around the block from Plymouth Church, to go to Annapolis. There they were employed searching for ships and arms that had been concealed by the Rebels and rebuilding a railroad. For the rest of their three-month enlistment, they were assigned to maintain order at Baltimore.

The Thirteenth was not enlisted for three-year service, although a number of its men volunteered for such duty with the Eighty-seventh Infantry Regiment in November 1861. In May 1862, the Thirteenth was again called to active service, this time serving at Suffolk, Virginia, near Norfolk. On a third occasion, it was called up and ordered to Harrisburg, Pennsylvania, following the Battle at Chancellorsville, and served there at the time of the Battle at Gettysburg.[147]

Also quartered at the armory on Cranberry Street near Henry Street was the Fourteenth Brooklyn Regiment, under the command of Colonel Alfred Wood, who had been elected in November 1860 to the board of aldermen and was its presiding officer. He resigned to prepare the regiment for active duty.

Two companies of the Fourteenth were recruited from Plymouth Church. Church members and the Beecher family helped equip the regiment. Beecher's home became a storehouse of military equipment. The church parlors became workshops where the women and girls of the congregation, under the direction of Mrs. Beecher, met daily to sew, knit and pack for the soldiers. They also did sewing for soldiers' wives.

Church members contributed to benevolence funds that were spent for clothing, blankets, pistols and holsters, as well as, in one instance, to help

Thirteenth Brooklyn Militia Regiment leaving the Cranberry Street Armory on the way to war, April 23, 1861, *Collection of Plymouth Church.*

bury a soldier's sister.[148] Mrs. Beecher personally solicited funds from church families and merchants. Beecher paid for equipment from his salary. He also had an account with the *Independent* because of his "Star articles." He used this account to purchase uniforms and equipment for the troops from Bowen's wholesale goods. In May 1861, Bowen presented him with a bill for $5,000 that he could not pay. In December 1861, Bowen used this leverage to persuade Beecher to accept the position of editor in chief of the *Independent*, as a means to pay off the debt.

Beecher was involved in all aspects of preparing the regiment for war. He preached a sermon on "The National Flag" to two companies of the regiment, many of them members of the church. On that day, church members contributed $3,000 to purchase equipment for the regiment. He preached another sermon, "The Camp, Its Dangers and Duties," directed to soldiers going to the front.[149]

Most of the regiment left Brooklyn on May 18, 1861, and initially served at Washington. At the First Battle of Bull Run, on July 21, 1861, the Fourteenth Brooklyn earned the nickname "Red Legged Devils" because of its distinctive uniforms. Referring to the regiment's colorful red trousers as the men repeatedly charged up Henry House Hill, Confederate general Stonewall Jackson yelled to his men, "Hold on Boys! Here come those red legged devils again!"

During the battle, Colonel Wood was wounded, captured and imprisoned. He was released and arrived in Brooklyn in February 1862. He was prevented from returning to his regiment because he was not fit for duty as a result of his wounds and imprisonment. In November 1863, Colonel Wood was elected mayor of Brooklyn, assuming his duties on January 1, 1864.[150]

In December 1861, New York State instituted numerical designations, and the Fourteenth became the Eighty-fourth New York Volunteer Infantry, but at the regiment's request and because of its service in the First Battle of Bull Run, the United States Army continued to recognize it as the Fourteenth Brooklyn. Even when the army battle dress uniform was standardized as blue, the regiment continued to wear the "Chasseur" uniform. Brooklyn paid to keep the unit in this uniform.

Over the next three years, the Fourteenth took part in the major battles of the Army of the Potomac. In the action in the cornfield at Antietam, the Fourteenth Brooklyn became known as the "Eastern Iron Brigade" because it held its ground with the "Black Hats" of the Sixth Wisconsin, known as the "Western Iron Brigade." Three monuments commemorating actions of the regiment are on the battlefield at Gettysburg. The regiment's last two battles were the Wilderness Campaign and at Spotsylvania Courthouse in General Grant's spring campaign in 1864. The unit was mustered out on May 25, 1864, at Fulton Ferry. During its three years of active service, 1,751 officers and men served in the regiment, and it sustained 717 killed, wounded and missing, or almost 41 percent of its men. Brooklyn historian Henry R. Stiles wrote in 1869, "The Fourteenth has the most glorious record of service during the war of any regiment in the militia, or of any regiment recruited especially for the war."[151]

According to the Beecher family biography, after the Thirteenth and Fourteenth Regiments had departed, Henry Ward Beecher "determined to be represented in the war by a whole regiment." Thus, he led the effort to organize the First Long Island Volunteers (known as the "Brooklyn Phalanx"), a regiment largely recruited from members of Plymouth Church. He took upon himself the "entire burden of equipping this unit." The family history noted, "This regiment would never have had any existence but for the labors of Mr. and Mrs. Beecher, and the members of the church whom they interested in it." Having already provided for two other regiments, church members contributed additional benevolence

Left: Colonel Alfred Wood, commanding officer of the Fourteenth Brooklyn Infantry Regiment in 1861. *Author's collection.*

Below: Alfred R. Waud, a Civil War illustrator for *Harper's Weekly*, made this drawing of a "skirmish between the Brooklyn Fourteenth and 300 Rebel cavalry" at the Battle of Sharpsburg or Antietam, as noted on the back of the paper. Historians have found no records that the regiment was engaged with cavalry at that battle. *Library of Congress.*

funds that were spent on clothing and equipment for the Brooklyn Phalanx. The Beechers' eldest son, Henry Barton Beecher, joined it and was commissioned a lieutenant. The regimental chaplain was James Chaplin Beecher, Henry Ward's youngest brother. James was discharged from the unit at Yorktown, Virginia, in September 1862. Later in the war, he was appointed to recruit an African American regiment at New Bern, North Carolina. He was commissioned a

James Chaplin Beecher, Henry Ward Beecher's younger brother, served as chaplain of the First Long Island Volunteers in 1861. He is pictured here in his later assignment as colonel in the First North Carolina Colored Volunteers. *Collection of Plymouth Church.*

colonel in the First North Carolina Colored Volunteers and mustered out as brevet brigadier general after the war ended.[152]

The Long Island Volunteers was mustered into service for three years on June 20 and 24, 1861, and received its numerical designation of the Sixty-seventh New York Infantry Regiment on August 19. Seven companies were from Brooklyn and one each from Allegany and Wayne Counties and Rochester. Company E was known as "Beecher's Pets."

The regiment was posted to defend Washington until March 1862, when it joined the advance under General McClellan in the Peninsula Campaign. It was engaged in the Battles of Chancellorsville and Gettysburg. A monument to the regiment is located on Culp's Hill at Gettysburg, where the unit was engaged on July 2 and 3. It served with the Army of the Potomac in Grant's spring campaign until the start of the Siege of Petersburg, when the original enlistments mustered out on July 4, 1864. Those who joined the unit later were consolidated with the Sixty-fifth New York Infantry and participated in General Sheridan's Shenandoah Valley Campaign in August and September 1864 before they returned to Petersburg, where they served through the end of the war.

NEW AMERICAN MISSIONARY ASSOCIATION MISSION

During the Civil War, Lewis Tappan and George Whipple directed American Missionary Association activities in Virginia and South Carolina that spread thereafter to other Southern states. Their work was a coordinated effort to bring

George Whipple. *Author's collection.*

freed people into American society by providing relief and establishing schools for them. George Whipple had been one of the Lane Theological Seminary "rebels" who participated in the debates led by Theodore Weld. After they were prevented from participating in antislavery activities, George and the others transferred to Oberlin College. Graduating from Oberlin, he was ordained and became professor of mathematics. When he took a position at the American Missionary Association, he moved to New York, lived in Brooklyn and joined Plymouth Church. Working at the low-paying position at the association, he had to sell his home. As corresponding secretary, he wrote thousands of letters of encouragement and occasionally a gentle rebuke to missionaries in the field. He was a workaholic, laboring at his office well past midnight and then wrapping himself in a blanket and sleeping on his desk before starting work again at dawn.[153]

Even though Fort Sumter fell to the Confederates, Fort Monroe at the southern tip of the Virginia Peninsula, bounded by the York and James Rivers and Chesapeake Bay, remained in Federal possession, with Major General Benjamin Butler of the Massachusetts militia commanding Union forces there. In May 1861, three enslaved men who had been working to construct Confederate fortifications nearby escaped at night and rode a skiff to Fort Monroe. The next day, a Confederate officer came to the fort under white flag of truce to demand their return under the Fugitive Slave Law of 1850. In response, General Butler refused, asserting that since Virginia claimed to be out of the Union, the Fugitive Slave Law did not apply. He declared that he had no obligation to return them as they were "contraband of war," or confiscated enemy property. Word of this spread among the enslaved people. The next day, eight more arrived, and on the following day, forty-seven appeared, including women and children. Thereafter, what started out as a trickle became a flood. By July, about one thousand fugitives had arrived at Fort Monroe.[154]

Over the course of ten days in August 1861, the mission of the American Missionary Association changed. Lewis Tappan wrote to General Butler to find out what the association could do for the contrabands. Starting out with an Underground Railroad mindset, he asked whether the association could assist by bringing the "self-emancipated" blacks north to the free states, where they could find employment and could be helped. General Butler replied that the contrabands were better off in Virginia. Tappan raised the concern that the blacks might be returned to slavery if they remained in the South. Then, after a short delay during which the association leadership was likely studying what to do, he asked the general whether someone could come to Fort Monroe to act as a missionary to the contrabands and to provide for their needs.[155]

Although General Butler said that the contrabands were being well cared for and that their religious needs were being met, the association sent Reverend Lewis C. Lockwood to Virginia to investigate their condition. Arriving in Hampton on September 3, he quickly concluded that the blacks were anxious for learning and wanted to go to school. Two weeks later, he and Mrs. Mary Peake opened a school for twenty students that would become the Hampton Normal and Agricultural Institute, the first school for freedmen. Over the next months, Reverend Lockwood and the association opened other schools in the area. On several occasions, Plymouth Church raised benevolence funds for the association for relief of the contrabands at Fort Monroe. Also, women at Plymouth did sewing for contrabands.[156]

Catherine Sarah Lawrence, a Plymouth member, redeemed a young enslaved girl in Virginia whom she named Fannie Virginia Casseopia Lawrence. Catherine had gone to Virginia to be a nurse in 1861 and probably was located in the Fort Monroe area. Born into slavery on May 1, 1858, Fannie was baptized at Plymouth Church on May 10, 1863. She grew up at Plymouth, after which she moved to Peekskill.[157]

Farther south, on November 7, 1861, ships of the U.S. Navy sailed into Port Royal Sound, South Carolina. When the ships bombarded defending artillery batteries, cotton plantation owners fled, leaving behind some ten thousand enslaved blacks who worked on the plantations. On the following day, Union soldiers landed and occupied the Sea Islands of South Carolina, including the city of Beaufort. This commenced what was called the "Port Royal Experiment."[158]

At the request of Lewis Tappan and George Whipple, Reverend Mansfield French went on a fact-finding mission to the Sea Islands to find out what the American Missionary Association could do for the blacks there.

Catherine Lawrence and her five-year-old adopted daughter, Fannie Virginia Casseopia Lawrence, who was baptized at Plymouth Church in May 1863. The photograph was taken at the Kellogg Brothers Studio in Hartford, Connecticut, with an unidentified African American woman. *Library of Congress.*

When he returned, Tappan and Whipple concluded that the challenge of providing relief and education at the Sea Islands was too much for the association to handle alone. As a result, they called a public meeting at Cooper Institute for February 20, 1862, at which those attending adopted resolutions to create the National Freedmen's Relief Association. In Boston, abolitionists also provided relief and teachers. The work provided a model for the support of freedmen during Reconstruction throughout the South.[159]

During the war years, the association's relief efforts and establishment of schools followed the progress of the Northern armies. As thousands of enslaved people fled to the Union lines seeking freedom, many found death instead because the army was not prepared to take care of them. In makeshift shelters, many died from disease, exposure and malnutrition. Lewis Tappan reported that by the end of 1863, about three thousand containers of goods and clothes for freed people had passed through his office. The Sewing Circle of Plymouth Church sent several bags or barrels almost monthly.[160]

Throughout the war, the American Missionary Association increased its teachers and missionaries. By 1862, the association had 18 teachers and missionaries in the South. By May 1863, the number had grown to 60 teachers and missionaries, teaching 4,000 pupils. In May 1864, the association had 180 teachers and missionaries at work and 250 in October, as the association was teaching 12,000 pupils in day schools, a similar number in Sabbath schools and thousands more in night schools. In mid-1865, the association continued to have 250 teachers and missionaries in the field. Seventeen days after the United States Army entered Richmond, the association had established schools there with a daily attendance of 1,500 students.

PLYMOUTH SUPPORTS EMANCIPATION

In 1861 and 1862, association leadership was discouraged by the lack of protection the army was providing blacks in the South. They blamed President Lincoln for failing to take care of "the suffering poor," as Lewis Tappan wrote in August 1862. When the president issued the preliminary Emancipation Proclamation one month later, Tappan thought that his prayers had been partially answered. He was ecstatic when the final proclamation was issued on January 1, 1863.[161]

Harriet Beecher Stowe traveled to Washington in December 1862 to encourage President Lincoln to issue the final proclamation as promised. He is reported to have greeted her with, "Is this the little lady who made this great war?" Lincoln was probably referring to the public response to *Uncle Tom's Cabin*. He may also have been recalling that he had borrowed *A Key to Uncle Tom's Cabin* in the summer of 1862, when he was wrestling with the decision to issue the preliminary Emancipation Proclamation.[162]

Celebrations for the final proclamation were held in many places in the North. At the one in Boston, Harriet Beecher Stowe was hailed. At an "Emancipation Jubilee" held at Cooper Institute in New York City, Lewis Tappan gave a short speech. It must have been a moving moment to see the seventy-five-year-old "patriarch" of the New York City abolitionist movement on that day. In his hand, he held a copy of the letter that John Quincy Adams had sent to him in March 1841, informing him that the Supreme Court had freed the *Amistad* captives and telling him, "Thanks in the name of humanity and justice to *you*." He talked about the path abolitionists had taken and that the proclamation did not go as far as he had hoped, but it promised complete abolition of slavery in the future. To cheers and laughter, he remarked that while some people questioned the ability of blacks to live in freedom, he believed that "a white man was as good as a black man, if he behaved himself."[163]

Henry Ward Beecher preached about the significance of the proclamation, and the *Independent*, of which he was editor in chief, hailed the event.

Sojourner Truth. *Collection of Plymouth Church.*

Because the president issued the Emancipation Proclamation under his war powers, the Thirteenth Amendment to the Constitution was necessary to end slavery when the war ended. The *Independent* participated in the campaign to achieve the amendment.

In early 1863, Harriet Beecher Stowe wrote an article, "Sojourner Truth: The Libyan Sibyl," for the *Atlantic Monthly*'s April issue. The article introduced Sojourner, who had traveled the lecture and reform circuit to the broader white American public. In the article, Harriet described Sojourner's 1853 visit to Harriet's Andover, Massachusetts, home at the time when her brother Henry was one of her houseguests. At that time, Harriet had written a "puff," which, since Harriet was the world's best-selling author, undoubtedly boosted the sales of *The Narrative of Sojourner Truth*, originally published in 1850. Harriet's endorsement became the introduction to Sojourner's 1853 edition of her *Narrative*.[164]

A year later, Sojourner decided that she would go to Washington, D.C., to meet President Lincoln, whom she called the "first Antislavery President." On the way to the nation's capital, she went through New York, and on October 2, she took the ferry to Brooklyn to hear Henry Ward Beecher's sermon that she called "a feast for her poor old soul." On that occasion, probably as a result of meeting her in 1853 and also of his sister's *Atlantic Monthly* article, Beecher invited her to speak to the congregation from his stage. On October 29, Sojourner met President Lincoln.[165] Five years later, in 1869, Sojourner spoke again at Plymouth Church on a visit through New York City.[166]

After the Emancipation Proclamation was issued, the claimed inferiority of black people became an obstacle to equal rights for freed people. Lewis Tappan asserted that equality before the law was "the Gospel rule" and that the "political salvation" of the United States depended on it. In May 1863, Theodore Tilton delivered a major speech at the annual meeting of the American Anti-Slavery Society entitled "The Negro." Tilton argued, "Looked at through the centuries, the question of races sinks into insignificance. The only generalization that will stand is, not that there are five races of men, or seven, or twelve, but only one—the universal human race in which all men are brothers, and God is father over all!"[167]

BEECHER ARGUES IN THE UNITED KINGDOM

In June 1863, Henry Ward Beecher left on a trip to Europe to get some rest. Some people criticized him for leaving when, as he said, "it was perhaps the dreariest period in the whole war." The Confederates had had a series of successes, including the stunning victory at Chancellorsville. When Beecher went to Europe, Theodore Tilton became acting editor in chief of the *Independent*. When Beecher returned, he did not continue as editor in chief. Bowen finally appointed Tilton to that position in 1864.[168]

When Beecher arrived in England, he was asked to speak in favor of the Union cause, but he refused and proceeded to the continent. Upon returning to Britain in October, Beecher learned of a movement to persuade Parliament to recognize the Confederacy. In response, he gave five speeches on various aspects of slavery to mostly hostile audiences in Manchester, Glasgow, Edinburgh, Liverpool and London.[169]

Upon Beecher's return, it was clear that the United Kingdom would not recognize the Confederacy and would remain neutral, thus cutting off military supplies the South desperately needed. Oliver Wendell Holmes wrote a summary of his speeches that was published under the title "The Minister Plenipotentiary" in the January 1864 issue of the *Atlantic Monthly*. He said that Beecher had "finished a more remarkable embassy than any envoy who has represented us in Europe since Franklin pleaded the cause of the young Republic at the Court of Versailles." General Robert E. Lee, according to his aide Roger Pryor, said that if it had not been for *Uncle Tom's Cabin* and Henry Ward Beecher's speeches in Britain, the Confederacy would have secured the recognition of the United Kingdom and France, with all that would have meant "in moral and material aid."[170]

Henry Ward Beecher in portrait, commemorating his sermon at the raising of the flag at the opening of Fort Sumter in April 1865. *Collection of Plymouth Church.*

President Lincoln told his cabinet that if the war were won, Beecher would be the man to raise the flag at Fort Sumter, "for without Beecher in England there might have been no flag to raise." Thus, in April 1865, the president asked Beecher to speak at the flag-raising at Fort Sumter, following General Lee's surrender of the Army of Northern Virginia. When Beecher was on his way home, he learned that Lincoln had been assassinated.

Five years after Abraham Lincoln was invited to speak at Plymouth Church, and as the Civil War was ending, Lincoln echoed his Cooper Institute words that "right makes might" in the final sentence of his Second Inaugural Address—one that Frederick Douglass said "sounded more like a sermon than a state paper." Lincoln noted, "With malice toward none; with charity for all; with firmness in the right, as God gives us to see the right, let us strive to finish the work we are in; to bind up the nation's wounds; to care for him who shall have borne the battle, and for his widow, and his orphan—to do all which may achieve and cherish a just, and a lasting peace, among ourselves, and with all nations."[171]

Since President Lincoln was assassinated a little over a month later, he did not implement his Second Inaugural Address to bring about Reconstruction of the Union. That would be left to others.

CHAPTER 8

STRIVING TO ACHIEVE EQUALITY

As Northern victory in the Civil War was approaching, Americans understood that the divided and war-torn nation would have to be rebuilt, a process called "Reconstruction." How that would take place, however, was not clear. President Lincoln made a plan for the state of Louisiana, but Congress rejected his proposed approach. He also set forth in his Second Inaugural Address the principle of "with malice toward none; with charity for all; with firmness in the right, as God gives us to see the right," with the goal to "achieve and cherish a just, and a lasting peace, among ourselves." But the goals of justice for freed people and generosity to former Confederates would be difficult to implement. How, for instance, would the reconstructed nation bring nearly 4 million newly freed black people into American society to live peacefully with about 6 million white Southerners, many of whom looked upon them as "inferior beings," described by Chief Justice Taney as "so inferior that they had no rights which a white man was bound to respect"?

Members of Plymouth Church participated in the arguments about rebuilding the United States. Henry Bowen was the owner and became publisher of the *Independent*, by then the largest and most influential political-religious weekly newspaper in the nation with a circulation of seventy thousand. The paper's editor in chief, Theodore Tilton, reported the political news and also commented on it in editorials. Not only was he a colleague and fellow Plymouth Church member with Bowen, Henry Ward Beecher, Lewis Tappan and George Whipple, but he also corresponded and

"Contrabands," photographed by Mathew Brady, shows seven formerly enslaved men dressed in old U.S. Army uniforms, standing in front of a wagon and a shack. *Library of Congress.*

consulted with William Lloyd Garrison, Wendell Phillips and Boston-based abolitionists. The staff of the paper changed in 1865, as Oliver Johnson, who had been coeditor of the *Anti-Slavery Standard*, the American Anti-Slavery Society journal, became managing editor, and Joshua Leavitt was assigned responsibility for the "Religious Intelligence" column. After 1865, the principles of the *Independent* were "justice and equality" for black people, American Indians, Chinese and women.[172]

Henry Ward Beecher said that he believed that Reconstruction would be "quick" and "easy." In his speech at Fort Sumter, he noted, "The moment their willing hand drops the musket and they return to their allegiance, then stretch out your own honest right hand to greet them." According to Laura Towne, one of the teachers in the South Carolina Sea Islands who talked with him after the speech, he explained, "One nation, under one government, without slavery, has been ordained, and shall stand. On this base Reconstruction is easy, and needs neither architect nor engineer."[173]

On March 3, 1865, understanding that the process required new means, Congress created the Freedmen's Bureau. On the recommendation of Secretary of War Edwin Stanton and of Henry Ward Beecher, President Andrew Johnson appointed to be commissioner of the bureau General Oliver O. Howard, the one-armed general who had commanded the right wing of General Sherman's March to the Sea through Georgia and the Carolinas.[174]

At the end of the war, the Freedmen's Bureau faced the enormous problem of providing relief in terms of food, clothes and shelter to millions of displaced black and white persons in the South who had been devastated by war, with armies living off the land. Even after vast effort, the bureau failed to relieve the poverty.[175]

PRESIDENTIAL RECONSTRUCTION

President Johnson went about Reconstruction quickly. As early as May 29, little more than six weeks after President Lincoln died, Johnson had granted amnesty to Confederate soldiers in North Carolina, "with restitution of all rights of property, except as to slaves." All returning Confederates had to do was to accept the laws, acknowledge the end of slavery and submit to federal authority. On June 13, when Mississippi received an identical Reconstruction proclamation, it was clear that President Johnson had a model for other former Confederate states.[176]

In May 1865, Theodore Tilton asserted in a series of editorials in the *Independent* that as conditions of Reconstruction of Southern states, blacks must be granted land and the right to vote. Concerned about President Johnson's Reconstruction policies, he continued to hope that the president might be persuaded to change, until October 1865, when he broke with the president and urged Congress to stop him.[177]

The president showed early on that he would not continue policies of the Lincoln administration. He overruled Reconstruction plans of the previous administration that benefited freed people in the South Carolina Sea Island experiment in which the American Missionary Association was active. On January 12, 1865, Secretary Stanton and General William T. Sherman met with twenty leaders of Savannah's black community concerning the welfare of freed people. Four days later, after Secretary Stanton had read and approved it, General Sherman issued his Special Order No. 15, in which he set aside the Sea

This photograph shows freed adults and children about to go into the field on the Hopkinson Plantation on Edisto Island, South Carolina. The woman standing next to the wheel of the cart has a heavy cotton hoe used on Sea Islands plantations as the sole means of cultivation, as plows were rarely used. *Library of Congress.*

Islands and land thirty miles inland from the ocean along the South Carolina and Georgia coasts for settlement by black families. The farms for the freed people were to be forty-acre plots, and he offered them broken-down mules that the army could no longer use, a plan that became known as "forty acres and a mule." By June, about forty thousand formerly enslaved people had settled on "Sherman's land." The American Missionary Association missionaries and teachers in the Sea Islands helped implement Sherman's order.[178]

In the summer of 1865, President Johnson overruled Sherman's order. He commanded federal land to be returned to former owners. In late October, General Howard of the Freedmen's Bureau traveled to the Sea Islands, on President Johnson's instructions, to inform freed people of the new policy. He was met with disbelief and protest. A committee petitioned the president, but to no avail. Thus, in South Carolina and Georgia, the army forcibly evicted black people who had settled on Sherman's land.[179]

When it convened in late 1865, Congress faced the rise of Southern opposition to the emancipation of formerly enslaved people. Southern states had passed "black codes" that were intended to regulate the lives of formerly enslaved people. In March 1866, Congress passed the Civil Rights Act of

1866, granting equality before the law to all Americans and making it a crime to deprive people of their civil rights. This was the first attempt to define what the freedom granted in the Thirteenth Amendment meant. When the bill was being debated, Theodore Tilton said that it was good as far as it went but that freedom would only be protected when people could vote. In a letter, Beecher urged President Johnson to sign it. The president vetoed the bill and then explained his veto in decidedly racist language. Theodore Tilton went to Washington to lobby for overriding the veto. In April, Congress overrode the veto. Thereafter in 1866, the president vetoed each Reconstruction bill passed by Congress, and Congress voted to override almost all of his vetoes.[180]

Fourteenth and Fifteenth Amendments

In June 1866, Congress approved and sent to the states for ratification the Fourteenth Amendment. This would incorporate into the Constitution provisions of the Civil Rights Act. It established the principle of citizenship for all persons born in the United States, thus repudiating Chief Justice Taney's statement in the *Dred Scott* case that no black person could be a United States citizen. It prohibited the states from denying people "life, liberty, or property, without due process of law" or denying them "equal protection of the laws." This was the constitutional guarantee of legal equality.

The Fourteenth Amendment did not grant blacks the right to vote. Theodore Tilton and other abolitionists expressed their disappointment that the amendment had not included suffrage.[181]

The Fourteenth Amendment became the central issue of the 1866 midterm elections. President Johnson made a series of speeches to urge voters to elect members of Congress who would support his Reconstruction policies. The president accused his opponents of intending to assassinate him. His erratic behavior was criticized. Riots in New Orleans and Memphis in which white policemen and citizens killed scores of black people caused further opposition.

At a convention of Southern and Northern Republicans in Philadelphia in early September, Theodore Tilton made an impact. Rochester Republicans had elected Frederick Douglass to be a delegate. Some Republicans were fearful that Douglass's attendance at the convention would hurt the party's chances in parts of the North where equality with freed people was unpopular. The delegates assembled at Independence Hall for a procession to National Hall. Delegates were supposed to walk two abreast. When it appeared that Douglass would have to walk alone, Theodore Tilton came up and locked arms with Douglass. The two of them marched down the streets together. Spectators cheered.

At the convention, when Tilton realized that Republicans could not win elections in the South unless black people voted, he led the New York delegation to pass a black suffrage resolution. Convention leadership prevented the suffrage issue from being discussed, but a Committee on Unreconstructed States endorsed black suffrage. Border-state delegates tried to adjourn the meeting. Tilton, Douglass and Anna Dickinson went to the platform and turned the convention into a popular meeting. Southerners made Tilton the chairman. Tilton, Douglass and Dickinson made speeches. The southerners were particularly interested in Dickinson, as they had never heard a woman speak in public. The following morning, the southerners met again and proposed a resolution endorsing black suffrage that was adopted. Observers agreed that the actions and speeches of Tilton, Douglass and Dickinson had achieved the result.[182]

During Reconstruction, Henry Ward Beecher and Henry Bowen's newspaper, the *Independent*, edited by Theodore Tilton, took different positions on policies. Beecher supported an easy and quick return of southern states to the Union, treating the former Confederates generously. The *Independent*, and especially Tilton, advocated federal government protection of freedmen. In the late summer of 1866, President Johnson held a convention in Cleveland. Henry Ward Beecher was invited to be the chaplain to the convention. He declined the invitation and sent a letter supporting the president. When the letter appeared in the press, it provoked criticism. Theodore Tilton attacked him in an editorial in the *Independent*. Beecher's response was defensive.[183]

In the elections in the fall of 1866, Republicans opposing the president's policies won landslide victories. As a result of his activities during the fall campaign, Theodore Tilton joined the leading abolitionist lecturers on tours of the Midwest in the winter of 1866–67, each delivering an average of one hundred speeches.[184]

After the presidential election of 1868, when General U.S. Grant won, Congress approved the Fifteenth Amendment to the Constitution, prohibiting anyone to deny any citizen the right to vote because of "race, color, or previous condition of servitude." Theodore Tilton wanted more, arguing for language that would prevent disenfranchisement by literacy or property qualifications. That proposal was turned down because several Northern states had such requirements, making ratification impossible.[185]

TEACHING FREED PEOPLE

A major part of the Reconstruction story was providing education to freed adults and children, most of whom were illiterate. This became the focus of the American Missionary Association during Reconstruction. From the time of its organization in 1846, Lewis Tappan had provided leadership of the American Missionary Association. At the end of 1865, when he was seventy-seven years old, Tappan announced his retirement, having concluded that his poor hearing made him unfit for his duties as treasurer and member of the executive committee. George Whipple took over Tappan's leadership role at the association.[186]

George Whipple and Freedmen's Bureau commissioner Howard worked closely together. The bureau's general superintendent of education, John W. Alvord, who had known Whipple since they were Lane Seminary "rebels" who left to go to Oberlin, introduced them, and within a few months of their meeting in September 1865, they had become good friends. Howard was impressed with Whipple's knowledge and experience with freed people and once called Whipple "my beau ideal of wisdom." He told an aid society that Whipple was "an excellent man to consult with, from his extensive and practical knowledge of the South."[187]

Soon after the war ended, the American Missionary Association worked closely with the Freedmen's Bureau to provide relief for the many newly freed black people who were in need of food, clothing and shelter. In many places throughout the South, black people lived in shacks or tents until they could find more permanent places to live.

In June 1865, a National Council of Congregational Churches met in Boston. The council recommended to Congregational churches that they raise $250,000 for work among the freedmen and designated the American Missionary Association as fit for the job that lay ahead. The association enlarged its staff and prepared for wider operations.

The association had short-term and long-range goals. During the war and early years of Reconstruction, the association and other freedmen's aid societies concentrated almost entirely on elementary education, hoping to make literate a large body of recently emancipated people. The association intended to turn elementary education over to state and local responsibility. This policy was very expensive and did little to diminish southern illiteracy. Secondary schools were also to be turned over to state and local responsibility, but public high schools for blacks developed slowly, and the association continued supporting them longer than anticipated.

Freedman's camp, photographed by Mathew Brady at the end of the Civil War, near Richmond, Virginia. *Library of Congress.*

The association's important long-term goal was to establish "permanent" institutions of higher education, colleges and universities. The project would take time to recruit faculty members, build facilities and attract able students. By 1866, the freedmen's associations realized that establishing schools to train black teachers for elementary grades, called normal schools, would be a more effective use of their finite resources. They sought to establish a graded secondary school or normal school in principal southern cities, although they never managed to do so.[188]

The association founded more than five hundred schools and colleges for the freedmen of the South during and after the Civil War, spending more money for that purpose than the Freedmen's Bureau. Plymouth Church members actively supported the association in the years from 1865 through 1874, contributing benevolence funds of $13,231 in the seven years for which there are records (almost $220,000 in 2012 dollars). In addition, Plymouth member Alfred E. Beach, who was editor of *Scientific American*, donated the money to the association to purchase the site of the Beach Institute that was named for him in Savannah, Georgia, and Plymouth member and trustee Rufus R. Graves gave a building and "valuable land" to the association for Talladega College in Talladega, Alabama. When Graves died in 1876, he bequeathed $100,000 "to be applied to the education of the colored people

This photograph of freed adults and children was taken circa 1862–65 outside a freedmen's school on Edisto Island in the Sea Islands, South Carolina. *Library of Congress.*

The interior of a freedmen's school. *Collection of Plymouth Church.*

in the southern states," $15,000 to the American Missionary Association and $10,000 to Berea College.[189]

Between 1866 and 1869, the association founded seven chartered schools, all of which were called colleges, although at first they were little more than high schools: Berea College in Kentucky (founded in 1855, closed in 1859 after John Brown's raid on Harpers Ferry and reopened in 1866), Atlanta University in Georgia (1865), Fisk University in Tennessee (1866), Talladega College in Alabama (1867), Hampton Institute in Virginia (1868), Straight University in Louisiana (1868) and Tougaloo College in Mississippi (1869). In addition, the association founded the theological department of Howard University in Washington, D.C. (1867), and thereby aided in the establishment of that school.

JUBILEE SINGERS AND SPIRITUALS

Founding chartered schools could be an adventure, as demonstrated at Fisk. In the fall of 1865, when the association decided to establish a freedmen's school in Nashville, Tennessee, General Clinton B. Fisk of the Freedmen's Bureau arranged to make an abandoned United States Army hospital complex available. He gave $30,000 to the school, while soliciting additional funds from his friends. The school was opened on January 9, 1866. Initially, it taught desperately needed black teachers. Two hundred enrolled immediately, and by the end of the first year, average daily attendance in primary school was at one thousand, ranging in age from seven to seventy. The administration was ambitious for the school and obtained incorporation as a university in August 1867, even though they did not have students of even normal grade level. Normal classes began shortly thereafter.

In 1871, Fisk was close to bankruptcy. The association was $78,000 in debt, with decreasing collections, because of declining northern interest in freedmen's problems. Also, midwestern charitable giving concentrated on Chicago after the Great Fire of 1871. The Freedmen's Bureau could not help because it had ended operations in 1870. Fisk and the association had planned to defray some of the expenses with tuition collections, but they could not collect much from poverty-ridden students.

To meet the school's precarious finances, a group of inexperienced student singers, led by an amateur musical director, proposed going on a singing tour

In 1866, the first buildings at Fisk University composed an abandoned military hospital complex. *Author's collection.*

The Fisk University Jubilee Singers went on tour to raise money for the school and came to Plymouth Church in 1871. *Library of Congress.*

to raise money for the school. Their first tour was a failure. The choir had sung familiar "white man's music" to white audiences, not yet comprehending the emotional, spiritual and musical impact—the great power—of what some called "slave songs." As they were singing music that some came to call "Songs of Jubilee," they adopted the name for themselves. The second tour took the newly named "Jubilee Singers" to New York City. Even though the American Missionary Association executive committee had been unwilling to endorse the tour as an official fundraiser for the school, George Whipple met with Henry Ward Beecher and persuaded him to invite the choir to sing at Plymouth Church's Friday evening prayer service on December 22, 1871.[190]

Beecher introduced them, saying that the congregation would hear "songs that have been sung by generations of benighted souls, on the plantation." The Singers started with the spiritual "Steal Away," a secret signal or code song that had been used by enslaved people to inform others that a conductor on the Underground Railroad had come to lead them to freedom:

> *Steal away, steal away, steal away to Jesus!*
> *Steal away, steal away home, I hain't got long to stay here!*

The Plymouth Church congregation was transfixed. After twenty minutes of singing, Beecher rose and said, "Folks can't live on air. Though they sing like nightingales, they need more to eat than nightingales do." The collection that night was $250.

Beecher invited them back for another concert, and other churches invited them to sing. By the end of December, the Singers were able to send their school $600. The American Missionary Association endorsed them and sent out a circular calling for fundraising of $20,000 for Fisk.

The singing at Plymouth Church launched the Jubilee Singers on a worldwide concert tour that included a concert for Queen Victoria. Altogether, they raised $150,000 for Fisk.[191]

Plymouth Church helped the Jubilee Singers of Fisk University introduce spirituals to white Americans and the world. After the Civil War and emancipation, "Steal Away" and other spirituals symbolized a new sense of community inclusive of all races. Spirituals formed the foundation on which African Americans experienced a unique and common identity, eventually leading to blues, jazz and gospel. Bernice Johnson Reagon said, "Spirituals record the struggle of a people to survive, but like no other histories, they also have the power to touch the souls and stir the emotions of the people who sing and hear them."[192]

EPILOGUE

Some abolitionists thought that their work was finished when emancipation took place. William Lloyd Garrison argued that the American Anti-Slavery Society should cease its work when the Thirteenth Amendment ending slavery was ratified. Wendell Phillips disagreed and persuaded the society to continue its work until the Fifteenth Amendment granted black men the vote. Only then did the society end its work on the grounds that it had achieved its purposes.[193]

George Whipple and the American Missionary Association decided that the mission to assist freed people in becoming educated in the South was not finished when the Fifteenth Amendment was ratified. He continued to lead the association until this death in 1876. During his last year, the association commenced the establishment of Tillotson Collegiate and Normal Institute in Austin, Texas. The association continued its distinct identity until 1999, when it became a division of the United Church of Christ.[194]

Other civil rights causes continued. When black men were given suffrage, women were not, and they were angry. Henry Ward Beecher and Theodore Tilton were active in the women's suffrage movement, each of them at one point leading a women's suffrage association. In addition, when Chinese workers on the West Coast were being discriminated against, Beecher took up their cause in sermons, speeches and articles. Nevertheless, in 1882, Congress passed the Chinese Exclusion Act.[195]

The *Independent*'s advocacy of civil rights for freedmen has not received the attention that it deserves as the story of Plymouth Church is told. For many years, Reconstruction was a subject that few people wanted to discuss. Americans were anxious to get on with their lives after the Civil War and its aftermath. Until recently, historians described Reconstruction in decidedly negative terms. Biographers of Beecher had little interest in studying the impact that Bowen and Tilton had on American history. Furthermore, in the early 1870s, Theodore Tilton sued Henry Ward Beecher for alienation of the affections of his wife. The civil lawsuit was the focus of enormous attention in the press and ended up with a hung jury and Tilton and Bowen leaving the church. The congregation knew Beecher, Bowen and Tilton and chose to believe Beecher, for membership during and after what was called a "scandal" remained large and active and did not decline. Indeed, Bowen's adult children and his family continued to be active members of the church after he left. Outside the church, the lawsuit did not seem to affect Beecher, as he continued to take lengthy lecture tours across the United States. Furthermore, in 1881, a San Francisco congregation tried to entice Beecher to leave Plymouth and become its minister, an invitation he declined.[196]

After Reconstruction, black and white abolitionists maintained their close relationships. Evidence of this comes from the attendance at funerals. When Lewis Tappan died in 1873, his funeral was held at Plymouth Church, with Henry Ward Beecher being joined on the platform by Reverend Amos Noah Freeman and Reverend James N. Gloucester, two black Presbyterian ministers. Reverend Charles B. Ray's attendance was noted by the *Brooklyn Daily Eagle*. When Reverend Ray died in August 1886, his funeral was held at his home, with Reverend Freeman pronouncing the eulogy and Beecher's assistant, Reverend S.B. Halliday, delivering a tribute because Beecher was out of town. Lewis Tappan's nephew and Reverend Dr. William Hayes Ward, an editor of the *Independent*, attended.[197]

Frederick Douglass had his own perspective on what needed to be accomplished and how long it would take. In December 1866, he spoke at Plymouth Church, calling for reconstructing "not merely the Southern States, but the very framework of the United States." He said that Americans should make "a government of the people, for the people and by the people and the whole people." He urged Americans to "blot out all discrimination against any class and every class who may be discriminated against" and also to "exclude no man from the ballot box because of his color; exclude no woman from the ballot box because of her sex; make it a government each for all and all for each, and there is no reason in the world why this republic of ours may not stand and flourish while the world stands."

Speaking a year after the Thirteenth Amendment to the Constitution ending slavery was ratified but before the Fourteenth and Fifteenth Amendments were ratified, Douglass warned Americans that the task of equality was not completed. He said, "An instant may be sufficient to snap the bondsman's chains, but a century is not sufficient to obliterate all traces of a former bondage."[198]

Just under a century after Frederick Douglass spoke at Plymouth, in February 1963, Reverend Dr. Martin Luther King Jr. addressed the congregation of Plymouth Church in a speech that would have an ending that he would repeat more than six months later at the Lincoln Memorial in Washington, D.C. Dr. King acknowledged that there had not yet been enough time to "obliterate all traces of a former bondage" that Frederick Douglass had talked about. He spoke about the "American Dream." He said that he used "this subject because America is essentially a dream—a dream yet unfulfilled. The substance of the dream is expressed in the sublime words of the Declaration of Independence—that 'all men are created equal.'"

Dr. King said that there are several things that need to be done to make this dream a reality: "[W]e have made of this world a neighborhood. We have failed to make of it a brotherhood…and now we must all learn to live together as brothers or we will perish together as fools. No individual can live alone; no nation can live alone…all life is inter-related and we are caught in an inescapable network of mutuality, tied in a single garment of destiny."

He continued, "[A]s we struggle in this continuing Struggle for Freedom and Justice, as we struggle to make the American dream a reality, we do not struggle alone; somehow the God of the Universe struggles with us."

He concluded, "With this faith we will be able to transform fatigue and despair into buoyancy of hope in bringing new light into the dark chambers of pessimism. And with this faith we will be able to struggle and make the American Dream a reality. With this faith we will be able to speed up the day when all God's children, black men and white men, Jews and Gentiles, Protestants and Catholics, will be able to join hands and sing in the words of the old Negro Spiritual, 'Free at Last, Free at Last, thank God Almighty we are Free at Last!'"[199]

Plymouth Church has had an impact on many people through the years. Branch Rickey and his wife were members and close friends of Plymouth's minister Reverend Dr. Wendell Fifield and his wife. One day in 1945, Rickey came to Fifield's study. Rickey told Fifield that he did not want to talk with him; he just wanted to be with him. So, Rickey paced around the room. He continued to do that, without talking, for about forty-five minutes. Finally, Rickey bent over Fifield's desk and cried, banging his fist, "I've got it!"

"Got what, Branch?" asked Fifield.

Rickey sank into a chair and said, "Wendell, I've decided to sign Jackie Robinson! Wendell, this was a decision so complex, so far reaching, fraught with so many pitfalls but filled with so much good, if it was right, that I just had to work it out in this room with you. I had to talk with God about it and be sure what He wanted me to do." That forty-five-minute talk with God in the warmth of Dr. Fifield's presence made American history.[200]

Plymouth Church has not forgotten its heritage. In 1997, the congregation celebrated the 150th anniversary of the founding of Plymouth Church with a weekend of events. On Friday evening, the church presented a concert entitled "A Celebration of Freedom: Moving People from Bondage to Freedom, Yesterday, Today, Tomorrow!" The concert featured the Plymouth Choir joined by two choirs of African American congregations, the Celestial Choir of the Bright Hope Baptist Church of Philadelphia and the Sanctuary Choir of the Convent Avenue Baptist Church of New York. On Saturday, reenactors of the Fourteenth Brooklyn Regiment staged a re-creation of the 1862 recruiting for the regiment. Also, on Saturday, historian Anthony Cohen gave a lecture on the Underground Railroad, describing his "Walk to Canada" in which he traveled 1,200 miles by foot, boat and rail from Maryland to Canada to retrace the footsteps of fugitives.

In 2005, the church presented a celebration of the publication of the *Plymouth Collection of Hymns and Tunes*, with the congregation hosting a musical evening entitled "Let Freedom Ring!" with African American choirs joining the Plymouth Choir in song and remembrance. The choirs were the Unity Choir of Mother AME Zion Church, the Brooklyn Ecumenical Choir of Bedford-Stuyvesant and a community chorus called Brooklyn Sings. Again, the Fourteenth Brooklyn Regiment reenactors participated. In 2010, these reenactors were joined by those of the Sixty-seventh New York Infantry, originally called the First Long Island Volunteers.

In 2012 and 2013, the congregation has found renewed interest in slavery, which today is called "human trafficking." Church members have invited speakers to talk about their work to rescue, educate and improve the lives of people caught up in human trafficking. Members hosted a conference with the Brooklyn District Attorney's Office. They are working with the international nongovernmental organization End Child Prostitution, Child Pornography and Trafficking (ECPAT), which combats the sexual trafficking of children. Church members have established an "Underground Thrift Store" that sells used clothing, decorative items and children's goods, giving a portion of the profits to an organization that works with women caught up in trafficking.

The children of Plymouth Church have adopted the Mission School of Hope in Cameroon, Africa, to provide the Baca tribe, formerly known as the Pygmies, with school and medical facilities.

Plymouth Church offers historical tours of its church buildings to help children and adults understand and envision slavery and the Underground Railroad. The United States National Park Service has designated the church as an Underground Railroad site of the "Network to Freedom" program. For the last several years, the church story has been told to more than four thousand schoolchildren and visitors each year, thereby preserving the memory of the long fight for freedom in which Plymouth Church played such an important role.

Notes

Introduction

1. Decker, "Working as a Team," *International Congregational Journal*, 33–42.
2. Garrison, "American Anti-Slavery Society, Declaration of Sentiments, December 6, 1833"; Genesis 1:26–27; Matthew 22:34–40; Mark 12:28–31; Luke 6:31; Acts 17:26–28; Galatians 3:28.

Prologue

3. Bruin and Hill to "the bearer" Paul Edmondson [*sic*], September 5, 1848, reprinted in Stowe, *Key to Uncle Tom's Cabin*, 164, and also in Pennington, *Fugitive Blacksmith*, 6–7.
4. Pennington, *Fugitive Blacksmith*, 7–8 (emphasis in original).
5. For Pennington's biography, see Webber, *American to the Backbone*.
6. Pennington, *Fugitive Blacksmith*, 6-7.
7. Ripley, *Black Abolitionist Papers*, 118; *Brooklyn Eagle*, June 23, 1848.
8. Stowe, *Key to Uncle Tom's Cabin*, 165.
9. Susan Howard to John H. Raymond, December 12, 1847, quoted in *Some Memories of John Tasker Howard*, 26–27.

10. *Rochester (New York) North Star*, November 17, 1848, quoted in Ricks, *Escape on the Pearl*, 191–92.
11. *Utica (New York) Liberty Press*, November 30, 1848, quoted in Ricks, *Escape on the Pearl*, 192.
12. Beecher and Scoville, *Biography of Henry Ward Beecher*, 292–93.
13. *Independent*, December 21, 1848.
14. For Leavitt's biography, see Davis, *Joshua Leavitt*; Lewis Tappan to Leavitt, December 9, 1846, Lewis Tappan Papers.

Chapter 1

15. *Some Memories of John Tasker Howard*, 23.
16. Stiles, *History of the City of Brooklyn*, 2:243; Weld, *Tower on the Heights*, 11, 14.
17. Howard, *Remembrance of Things Past*, 38–39; Thompson, *History of Plymouth Church*, 27. Copy of Contract for Purchase of Property, dated June 11, 1846, between First Presbyterian Church of Brooklyn and John T. Howard, signed by C.P. Smith for the Presbyterian Church, together with associated receipts and the deed to Plymouth Church, dated June 1, 1848, are inscribed at the beginning of *Plymouth Church Trustees and Annual Meeting Minutes, 1847–1932*; Statement of Thomas G. Shearman, quoted in *Some Memories of John Tasker Howard*, 28.
18. Beecher's introduction of William Cutter at twenty-fifth anniversary ceremonies in 1872, quoted in Thompson, *History of Plymouth Church*, 203; Elsmere, *Henry Ward Beecher*, 280–81.
19. According to Thompson, *History of Plymouth Church*, 28, the location of Beecher's speech was changed, and he addressed the Foreign Missionary Society. See also Abbott, *Henry Ward Beecher*, 73.
20. Knox, *Life and Work of Henry Ward Beecher*, 458.
21. Thompson, *History of Plymouth Church*, 8–61; meeting of June 11, 1847, *Plymouth Church Membership: Baptisms, Dismissions, Membership*, 1847–1865; meeting of June 14, 1847, *Plymouth Church Trustees and Annual Meeting Minutes, 1847–1932*. On September 27, 1847, the certificate of incorporation was recorded in the King's County Clerk's Office.
22. Housley, "The Independent," 29; Howard, *Life of Henry Ward Beecher*, 171; acceptance in Plymouth Church minutes, set forth in Thompson, *History of Plymouth Church*, 61, 62.

23. Statement of John Tasker Howard, quoted in Howard, *Life of Henry Ward Beecher*, 130.

24. Ibid., 131–32.

25. Abbott, *Henry Ward Beecher*, 75; Thompson, *History of Plymouth Church*, 62. As minister in Indianapolis, Indiana, Beecher had preached three sermons in which he "declared slavery an institution in defiance to the laws of God, and an outrage upon the rights of man." Elsmere, *Henry Ward Beecher*, 177, 260–66.

26. *New York Tribune*, June 2, 1853, quoted in Gossard, "New York Congregational Cluster," 105; Abbott, *Henry Ward Beecher*, 159.

27. Howard, *Life of Henry Ward Beecher*, 137; Thompson, *History of Plymouth Church*, 24–25; Jackson, *Encyclopedia of New York City*, 149.

28. Howard, *Life of Henry Ward Beecher*, 140–41; Beecher and Scoville, *Biography of Henry Ward Beecher*, 229–32.

29. *Brooklyn Eagle*, January 15, 1849.

30. Meeting of January 20, 1849, *Plymouth Church Trustees and Annual Minutes, 1847–1932*.

31. Meeting of February 3, 1849, *Plymouth Church Trustees and Annual Minutes, 1847–1932*, lease, March 1, 1849; *Brooklyn Star*, March 25, 1849.

32. Thompson, *History of Plymouth Church*, 68, 160.

33. See, generally, Kilde, *When Church Became Theatre*.

Chapter 2

34. Douglass, *Autobiographies*, 90.

35. Foner, *Business & Slavery*, 4–9.

36. U.S. Constitution, Art. IV, § 2, cl. 3.

37. Ray, *Sketch of the Life*, 30–31.

38. For Ruggles's biography, see Hodges, *David Ruggles*.

39. Wyatt-Brown, *Lewis Tappan*, 329–30.

40. For Ray's biography, see Ray, *Sketch of the Life*.

41. Still, *Underground Railroad*, 2:329; Tappan, *Life of Arthur Tappan*, 369.

42. Still, *Underground Railroad*, 2:331–32.

43. Ibid., 2:328–29.

44. Ray, *Sketch of the Life*, 45–46.

45. Still, *Underground Railroad*, 2:330.

46. Ray, *Sketch of the Life*, 35.

47. Webber, *American to the Backbone*, 318–19; *New York Times*, *Lemmon* case arguments before the Court of Appeals, January 25 and 26, 1860; *New York Times*, *Lemmon* case decision, April 26, 1860; *New York Tribune*, Louis Napoleon obituary, March 30, 1881, identifying acquaintance with Gerrit Smith, Arthur and Lewis Tappan and, later, Horace Greeley, Henry Ward Beecher and George William Curtis.

48. *Brooklyn Eagle*, October 4, 1872; Thompson, *History of Plymouth Church*, 77, 79.

49. American Missionary Association, *History*, 46–48.

50. William Still's version of the story is in Still, *Underground Railroad*, 1:185–99; Lewis Tappan's version is in Still, *Underground Railroad*, 2:334–36; Charles B. Ray's version is in Ray, *Sketch of the Life*, 36–45; a summary of their story is in Harrold, *Subversives*, 203–24.

51. Still, *Underground Railroad*, 2:334–36.

52. Ray, *Sketch of the Life*, 33; *New York State Vigilance Committee Annual Report, May 1950*, quoted in Barton, *Randolph Epistles*, 3; Abel and Klingberg, *Sidelight on Anglo-American Relations*, 247, n. 225; Campbell, *Slave Catchers*, 7; Quarles, *Black Abolitionists*, 154, 280, n. 28; Lewis Tappan to J. Smith, March 2, 1857, letterbook, Lewis Tappan Papers.

Chapter 3

53. Barton, *Randolph Epistles*, 3.

54. Speech of January 29, 1850, quoted in Bordewich, *America's Great Debate*, 135.

55. *Journal of Commerce*, December 12, 1849; January 8, 10, 12–16; March 6; June 27, 1850.

56. Beecher, "Shall We Compromise?" *Independent*, February 21, 1850, reprinted in Howard, *Patriotic Addresses*, 174.

57. *Independent*, "Mr. Clay's New Compromise," February 14, 1850; *Independent*, "Slave Trade at Washington," December 14, 1848; *Independent*, "How to Oppose the Fugitive Slave Law," October 24, 1850; *Independent*, "Establishing Slavery by Compromise," January 25, 1849; Housley, "The Independent," 90–97, 128.

58. *Brooklyn Eagle*, October 24, 1849; Beecher, "Shall We Compromise?" *Independent*, February 21, 1850, reprinted in Howard, *Patriotic Addresses*, 171, citing Acts, 4:19.

59. Ward, *Autobiography of a Fugitive Negro*, 81.

60. Beecher, "Law and Conscience," *Independent*, November 1, 1850.

61. Lewis Tappan to John Scoble, April 24, 1850, reprinted in Abel and Klingberg, *Sidelight on Anglo-American Relations*, 241, Wyatt-Brown, *Lewis Tappan*, 329.

62. *New York Globe*, reprinted in *Express*, May 10, 1850, quoted in Foner, *Business & Slavery*, 28.

63. *Brooklyn Eagle*, May 9, 1850; Lewis Tappan to John Scoble, May 25, 1850, reprinted in Abel and Klingberg, *Sidelight on Anglo-American Relations*, 241.

64. Howard, *Patriotic Addresses*, 84; see Tappan, *Life of Arthur Tappan*, 310–11.

65. Quoted in Potter and Fehrenbacher, *Impending Crisis*, 128 (emphasis in original).

66. Campbell, *Slave Catchers*, 25; American Missionary Association, 1850 Annual Report, 11, quoted in Brownlee, *New Day Ascending*, 98.

67. Beecher, "Fugitive Slave Bill at Its Work," *Independent*, October 3, 1850.

68. Tappan, *Fugitive Slave Bill*, 2–6, 21, 31, 35–36.

69. *Brooklyn Eagle*, September 25, 26 and 28, 1850.

70. *Brooklyn Eagle*, October 31, 1850; Foner, *Business & Slavery*, 44; New York Union Safety Committee, *Proceedings of the Union Meeting*; Beecher and Scoville, *Biography of Henry Ward Beecher*, 247.

71. Beecher and Scoville, *Biography of Henry Ward Beecher*, 147; *New York Tribune*, October 28, 1850, and *New York Post*, October 26, 29, 1850, quoted in Foner, *Business & Slavery*, 45.

72. Beecher and Scoville, *Biography of Henry Ward Beecher*, 247; Foner, *Business & Slavery*, 44–45.

73. Housley, "The Independent," 32, 37–38; Foner, *Business & Slavery*, 45, n. 57.

74. Gossard, "New York Congregational Cluster," 71; Housley, "The Independent," 37–38.

75. *Independent*, January 2 and 6, 1851; Foner, *Business & Slavery*, 60–61.

76. Lewis Tappan to John Scoble, April 3, 1851, reprinted in Abel and Klingberg, *Sidelight on Anglo-American Relations*, 259.

77. *Douglass' Paper*, October 16, 1851.

78. Foner, *Business & Slavery*, 69–79.

CHAPTER 4

79. H.B. Stowe to H.W. Beecher, February 1, 1851, Beecher Family Papers, Yale.

80. H.B. Stowe to C.E. Stowe, January 12, 1851, Stowe-Day Library; Harrold, *Gamaliel Bailey*, 142.

81. H.B. Stowe to C.E. Stowe, January 27 [1851], quoted in Hedrick, *Harriet Beecher Stowe*, 206; H.B. Stowe to H.W. Beecher, February 1, 1850, Beecher Family Papers, Yale; C.E. Stowe, *Life*, 145, quoted in Hedrick, *Harriet Beecher Stowe*, 207.

82. H.B. Stowe to Gamaliel Bailey, March 9, 1851, transcript in Garrison Papers at Boston Public Library, quoted in Reynolds, *Mightier than the Sword*, xiii.

83. Ibid.

84. Stowe, *Key to Uncle Tom's Cabin*, 22–23; Stowe, *Uncle Tom's Cabin*, 97–101.

85. H.B. Stowe to Seventh Earl of Carlisle, January 6, 1853, quoted in Reynolds, *Mightier than the Sword*, 130.

86. Lewis Tappan to P.J. Bolton, June 15, 1852, Abel and Klingberg, *Sidelight on Anglo-American Relations*, 296; resolution at Annual Meeting of American & Foreign Anti-Slavery Society, May 11, 1852.

87. Garrison, *Liberator*, March 26, 1852.

88. *Douglass' Paper*, April 20, 1853.

89. Stowe, *Uncle Tom's Cabin*, 67–68; Reynolds, *Mightier than the Sword*, xi.

90. Hedrick, *Harriet Beecher Stowe*, 213–14.

91. Stowe, *Uncle Tom's Cabin*, 142.

92. Ibid., 13.

93. *National Era*, August 1, 1850.

94. *Douglass' Paper*, April 1, 1852.

95. McCray, *Author of Uncle Tom's Cabin*, 106, quoted in Reynolds, *Mightier than the Sword*, 169.

96. Stowe, *Key to Uncle Tom's Cabin*, iii.

97. Quoted in Barnes, *Anti-Slavery Impulse*, 231.

98. Stowe, *Key to Uncle Tom's Cabin*, 5, 67, 121.

99. Ibid., 155–68. In the summer of 1852, Harriet helped Mary and Emily to attend the Young Ladies' Preparatory School at Oberlin College. Mary died there of tuberculosis in May 1853. Emily returned to Washington, where she worked at the school of Myrtilla Miner. Emily married in 1860 and died in 1895. Ricks, *Escape on the Pearl*, 248, 255, 264, 279.

100. *New York Tribune*, reprinted in the *Anti-Slavery Standard* of August 1853, quoted in Reynolds, *Mightier than the Sword*, 300, n. 146; Garrison, *Liberator*, September 8, 1853 (emphasis in original).

101. Foster, "Poor Uncle Tom, Good Night."

102. Senior, *American Slavery*, 29; see Von Frank, *Trials of Anthony Burns*, 197–219; Reynolds, *Mightier than the Sword*, 147.

103. Still, *Underground Railroad*, 2:329.

CHAPTER 5

104. Tappan to L.A. Chamerovzow, in Abel and Klingberg, *Sidelight on Anglo-American Relations*, 347–48.
105. New York Radical Political Abolitionists, *Proceedings of the Convention*; Tappan to L.A. Chamerovzow, in Abel and Klingberg, *Sidelight on Anglo-American Relations*, 358–59.
106. Stauffer, *Black Hearts*, 9, 10, 155; New York Radical Political Abolitionists, *Proceedings of the Convention*, 57, 64–65.
107. Stauffer, *Black Hearts*, 13–14.
108. H.B. Stowe to H.W. Beecher, January 13, 1854, Stowe Center; *Independent*, February 23, 1854; Hedrick, *Harriet Beecher Stowe*, 257; Beecher and Scoville, *Biography of Henry Ward Beecher*, 273–77.
109. Isely, "Sharps Rifle Episode," 552; Etcheson, *Bleeding Kansas*, 38.
110. Beecher, "Defence of Kansas," *Independent*, February 14, 1856.
111. *New York Tribune*, February 8, 1856.
112. Knox, *Life and Work of Henry Ward Beecher*, 160; *New York Tribune*, February 8, 1856; *Brooklyn Eagle*, September 16, 1856.
113. Applegate, *Most Famous Man*, 281–82; Pantle, "Connecticut Kansas Colony."
114. Beecher and Scoville, *Biography of Henry Ward Beecher*, 283; Abbott, *Henry Ward Beecher*, 211.
115. Thompson, *History of Plymouth Church*, 82–83.
116. *Independent*, June 1, 1856; Curran, *Peekskill's African American History*, 42.
117. Potter and Fehrenbacher, *Impending Crisis*, 218–19; McPherson, *Ordeal by Fire*, 105; Watts, "How Bloody," 123; Etcheson, *Bleeding Kansas*, 89–138.
118. King, "Henry Ward Beecher's Work for Congregational Singing," 137; Rigler, "John Zundel," 86.
119. Howard, *Life of Henry Ward Beecher*, 273.
120. *Some Memories of John Tasker Howard*, 32; *Brooklyn Eagle*, "The Religious Test in Politics," September 16, 1856, 2.

CHAPTER 6

121. *Dred Scott v. Sandford*, 19 U.S. 393 (1857).
122. This section of the opinion is at pages 403–27; Fehrenbacher, *Dred Scott Case*, 341.

123. U.S. Constitution, Article IV, § 3; U.S. History, Republican Platform, 1856, resolution 3.

124. Swisher, *Taney Period*, 632, 637, 650.

125. Fehrenbacher, *Dred Scott Case*, 431–35; *Independent*, "New Era," March 12, 1857; *Independent*, "The Reach of the Decision," March 26, 1857; *Radical Abolitionist*, "Decision of the Supreme Court," April 1857; *Radical Abolitionist*, "Fate of the 'Limitation' Policy," August 1857.

126. Lincoln speech on June 16, 1858, Fehrenbacher, *Lincoln: Speeches and Writings*, 1:432; Webber, *American to the Backbone*, 319.

127. *Brooklyn Eagle*, "Fugitive Slave Case in Brooklyn," December 2–5, 1857.

128. Swisher, *Taney Period*, 649.

129. Thompson, *History of Plymouth Church*, 22.

130. Ibid., 160.

131. Ibid. In 1857, the church revised its membership list, so the net increase was 378, bringing the total membership to 1,241. See also Member of the Church, *Memorial of the Revival*.

132. Thompson, *History of Plymouth Church*, 93.

133. Ibid., 98–108.

134. Housley, "The Independent," 135; McPherson, *Battle Cry of Freedom*, 210.

135. Knox, *Life and Work of Henry Ward Beecher*, 157.

136. American Missionary Association, "Missionary Boards in relation to Slavery, Caste, and Polygamy."

137. *Brooklyn Eagle*, January 26, 1860; Tilton, "American Board and American Slavery" speech.

138. Treasurer's reports reported the purchases of freedom from 1858 to 1860 of the following: (1) 1858—"Lewis Smith (colored) to buy his child," $300.00; (2) 1859—"Ellen Mitchell and children (slaves)," for $466.74; (3) 1860—money was paid for "a colored woman [Maus A. Douglas] to bring her child out of slavery," $252.12; (4) November 1860—Louisa Monroe, slave girl ($850.00); and (5) 1860—gave money to "colored man to bring his children from slavery," $85.00. *Plymouth Church Trustees and Annual Meeting Minutes, 1847–1932*, 212, 218, 224–26.

139. Fehrenbacher, *Lincoln: Speeches and Writings*, 2:118.

140. Holzer, *Lincoln at Cooper Union*, 5, 218–19, 243–44; Corry, *Lincoln at Cooper Union*, 10, 186–97.

141. Central Pacific Railroad Photographic History Museum, Republican Platform, 1860, paragraphs 7 and 8.

142. McPherson, *Struggle for Equality*, 25; Field, *Politics of Race*, 127–29.

143. McPherson, *Struggle for Equality*, 26.

Chapter 7

144. Foner, *Business & Slavery*, 198, 222–23; Housley, "The Independent," 46–47; *Brooklyn Eagle*, February 25, 1896.

145. McPherson, *Struggle for Equality*, 31–36; Richardson, *Christian Reconstruction*, 3.

146. Treasurer's report, *Plymouth Church Trustees and Annual Meeting Minutes, 1847–1932*, 234–39.

147. Stiles, *History of the City of Brooklyn*, 3:949–51.

148. Treasurer's report, *Plymouth Church Trustees and Annual Meeting Minutes, 1847–1932*, 234–43.

149. Howard, *Patriotic Addresses*, 289, 304.

150. Stiles, *History of the City of Brooklyn*, 2:455–58.

151. Tevis, *History of the Fighting Fourteenth*, 142–43; Stiles, *History of the City of Brooklyn*, 3:951.

152. Beecher and Scoville, *Biography of Henry Ward Beecher*, 317; treasurer's report, *Plymouth Church Trustees and Annual Meeting Minutes, 1847–1932*, 234–43.

153. Hollyday, *On the Heels of Freedom*, 18–19.

154. McPherson, *Battle Cry of Freedom*, 355–56; Newby-Alexander, *Hampton Roads*, 23–31.

155. Rose, *Rehearsal for Reconstruction*, 13; Wyatt-Brown, *Lewis Tappan*, 339; Richardson, *Christian Reconstruction*, 3–4.

156. Beard, *Crusade of Brotherhood*, 121; treasurer's report, *Trustees Minutes*, 236.

157. Curran, *Peekskill's African American History*, 43.

158. Rose, *Rehearsal for Reconstruction*, 17–18, 336.

159. Ibid., 26–27.

160. Richardson, *Christian Reconstruction*, 57–61, 64.

161. Ibid., 8.

162. McPherson, *Battle Cry of Freedom*, 89–90.

163. Richardson, *Christian Reconstruction*, 8–9; Wyatt-Brown, *Lewis Tappan*, 212, 337–38.

164. Painter, *Sojourner Truth*, 130–31, 151–63; Hedrick, *Harriet Beecher Stowe*, 270.

165. Pauli, *Her Name Was Sojourner Truth*, 210; Painter, *Sojourner Truth*, 200–207.

166. Washington, *Sojourner Truth's America*, 350.

167. Wyatt-Brown, *Lewis Tappan*, vii–viii, 337; Richardson, *Christian Reconstruction*, 20–22, 88–89; Tilton, "The Negro" speech, 8.

168. Beecher and Scoville, *Biography of Henry Ward Beecher*, 397; McPherson, *Struggle for Equality*, 38.

169. Beecher and Scoville, *Biography of Henry Ward Beecher*, 396–442.

170. *New York Times*, November 4, 1863; Howard, *Patriotic Addresses*, 422; Stowe, *Saints, Sinners and Beechers*, 293.

171. Douglass, *Autobiographies*, 801; Fehrenbacher, *Lincoln: Speeches and Writings*, 2:687.

CHAPTER 8

172. McPherson, *Struggle for Equality*, 87–88; Housley, "The Independent," 180–82.

173. Beecher and Scoville, *Biography of Henry Ward Beecher*, 454 (emphasis in original); Rose, *Rehearsal for Reconstruction*, 344.

174. Rose, *Rehearsal for Reconstruction*, 339.

175. Richardson, *Christian Reconstruction*, 57–62, 64.

176. McPherson, *Struggle for Equality*, 320–21; Rose, *Rehearsal for Reconstruction*, 349–50.

177. *Independent*, May 4, 11, 25, 1865; McPherson, *Struggle for Equality*, 320, 329–30, 335, 339.

178. Sherman, *Memoirs*, 2:245–52; Rose, *Rehearsal for Reconstruction*, 320–30.

179. Rose, *Rehearsal for Reconstruction*, 346–77; Foner, *Give Me Liberty*, 475–76, 483.

180. *Independent*, February 8, 1866; Applegate, *Most Famous Man*, 360.

181. McPherson, *Struggle for Equality*, 354.

182. Ibid., 360–63.

183. Applegate, *Most Famous Man*, 362.

184. McPherson, *Struggle for Equality*, 367.

185. *Independent*, February 11, 1869.

186. Richardson, *Christian Reconstruction*, 91–92.

187. Ibid., 76–77.

188. McPherson, *Struggle for Equality*, 406; Richardson, *Christian Reconstruction*, 123; American Missionary Association, *History*, 25–34.

189. Drake, "American Missionary Association," 198; treasurer's reports, *Plymouth Church Trustees and Annual Meeting Minutes, 1847–1932*; American Missionary Association, *History*, 29, 37; *Brooklyn Eagle*, September 15, 1876.

190. Ward, *Dark Midnight*, 152.

191. Ibid., 153–54.

192. Reagon, *We'll Understand It Better*, 13.

EPILOGUE

193. Mayer, *All on Fire*, 594, 613.

194. American Missionary Association, *History*, 34–35; Wikipedia, "American Missionary Association."

195. Applegate, *Most Famous Man*, 384, 387–88.

196. Membership list, 1847–1902, Plymouth Archives. In the summer of 1881, for instance, Beecher left Brooklyn on July 9 and ended in San Francisco on September 1, schedule, Plymouth Archives.

197. *Brooklyn Eagle*, June 25, 1873; Wyatt-Brown, *Lewis Tappan*, 342; Ray, *Sketch of the Life*, 60.

198. *Brooklyn Eagle*, December 18, 1866.

199. M.L. King address at Plymouth Church, February 10, 1963, Plymouth Church Archives.

200. Memorandum of June Fifield, Plymouth Church Archives.

BIBLIOGRAPHY

BOOKS, ARTICLES AND CASES

Abbott, Lyman. *Henry Ward Beecher*. Boston: Houghton Mifflin, 1903. Facsimile of the first edition with an introduction by William G. McLoughlin, New York: Chelsea House, 1980.

Abel, Annie Heloise, and Frank J. Klingberg, eds. *A Sidelight on Anglo-American Relations, 1839–1858: Furnished by the Correspondence of Lewis Tappan and Others with the British and Foreign Anti-Slavery Society*. Washington, D.C.: Association for the Study of Negro Life and History, 1927.

American and Foreign Anti-Slavery Society. *Twelfth Annual Report of the American and Foreign Anti-Slavery Society, Presented at New-York, May 11, 1852, with the Addresses and Resolutions*. New York: American and Foreign Anti-Slavery Society, 1852.

American Missionary Association. *History of the American Missionary Association, with Illustrative Facts and Anecdotes*. New York: Bible House, 1891. Facsimile of first edition, Charleston, SC: BiblioBazaar.

———. "Missionary Boards in Relation to Slavery, Caste, and Polygamy." *American Missionary Extra* (May 1854). Facsimile of first edition, Cornell University Library Digital Collections.

Applegate, Debby. *The Most Famous Man in America: The Biography of Henry Ward Beecher*. New York: Doubleday, 2006.

Barnes, Gilbert Hobbs. *The Anti-Slavery Impulse: 1830–1844*. Washington, D.C.: American Historical Association, 1933. Reprint with an introduction by William G. McLoughlin, New York: Harcourt, Brace & World, 1964.

Barton, Seth. *The Randolph Epistles*. Washington, D.C.: 1850. Facsimile of first edition, Cornell University Library Digital Collections.

Beard, Augustus Field. *A Crusade of Brotherhood: A History of the American Missionary Association*. Boston, MA: Pilgrim Press, 1909.

Beecher, Charles. *The Duty of Disobedience to Wicked Laws: A Sermon on the Fugitive Slave Law*. New York: John A. Gray, 1851. Facsimile of first edition, Cornell University Library Digital Collections.

Beecher, William C., and Samuel Scoville, assisted by Mrs. Henry Ward Beecher. *A Biography of Henry Ward Beecher*. New York: Charles L. Webster, 1888.

Bordewich, Fergus M. *America's Great Debate: Henry Clay, Stephen A. Douglas, and the Compromise that Preserved the Union*. New York: Simon & Schuster, 2012.

———. *Bound for Canaan: The Underground Railroad and the War for the Soul of America*. New York: Amistad, 2005.

Brownlee, Fred L. *A New Day Ascending*. Boston, MA: Pilgrim Press, 1946.

Burrows, Edwin G., and Mike Wallace. *Gotham: A History of New York City to 1898*. New York: Oxford University Press, 1999.

Campbell, Stanley W. *The Slave Catchers: Enforcement of the Fugitive Slave Law, 1850–1860*. Chapel Hill: University of North Carolina Press, 1970.

Central Pacific Railroad Photographic History Museum. Republican Platform, 1860. http://cprr.org/Museum/Ephemera/Republican_Platform_1860.html.

Corry, John A. *Lincoln at Cooper Union: The Speech that Made Him President*. Bloomington, IN: Xlibris Corporation, 2003.

Curran, John J. *Peekskill's African American History: A Hudson Valley Community's Untold Story*. Charleston, SC: The History Press, 2008.

Davis, Hugh. *Joshua Leavitt: Evangelical Abolitionist*. Baton Rouge: Louisiana State University Press, 1990.

DeBoer, Clara Merritt. *Be Jubilant My Feet: African American Abolitionists in the American Missionary Association, 1839–1861*. New York: Garland, 1994.

Decker, Frank. "Working as a Team: Henry Ward Beecher and the Plymouth Congregation in the Anti-Slavery Cause." *International Congregational Journal* 8, no. 2 (Fall 2009): 33–42.

Douglass, Frederick. *Autobiographies: Narrative of the Life, My Bondage and My Freedom, Life and Times*. Reprint, New York: Library of America, 1994.

Drake, Richard Bryant. "The American Missionary Association and the Southern Negro, 1861–1888." PhD diss., Emory University, 1957.

Dred Scot v. Sandford, 19 U.S. 393 (1857).

Elsmere, Jane Shaffer. *Henry Ward Beecher: The Indiana Years, 1837–1847*. Indianapolis: Indiana Historical Society, 1973.

Etcheson, Nicole. *Bleeding Kansas: Contested Liberty in the Civil War Era*. Lawrence: University Press of Kansas, 2004.

Fehrenbacher, Don E. *The Dred Scott Case: Its Significance in American Law and Politics*. New York: Oxford University Press, 1978.

Fehrenbacher, Don E., ed. *Lincoln: Speeches and Writings*. 2 vols. New York: Library of America, 1989.

Field, Phyllis F. *The Politics of Race in New York: The Struggle for Black Suffrage in the Civil War Era*. Ithaca, NY: Cornell University Press, 1982.

Foner, Eric. *Give Me Liberty! An American History*. New York: W.W. Norton, 2006.

Foner, Philip S. *Business & Slavery: The New York Merchants & the Irrepressible Conflict*. Chapel Hill: University of North Carolina Press, 1941.

Foster, Stephen. "Poor Uncle Tom, Good Night." From sketchbook of songs that Foster kept in 1850s. *Uncle Tom's Cabin* and American Culture, University of Virginia. http://utc.iath.virginia.edu/songs/kyhomef.html.

Garrison, William Lloyd. "American Anti-Slavery Society Declaration of Sentiments, December 6, 1833." *Selections from the Writings of W.L. Garrison*. Boston, MA: R.F. Wallcut, 1852. http://utc.iath.virginia.edu/abolitn/abeswlgct.html.

Gossard, John Harvey. "The New York Congregational Cluster, 1848–1871: Congregationalism and Antislavery in the Careers of Henry Ward Beecher, George B. Cheever, Richard S. Storrs and Joseph P. Thompson." PhD diss., Bowling Green State University, 1986.

Harrold, Stanley. *Gamaliel Bailey and Anti-Slavery Union*. Kent, OH: Kent State University Press, 1986.

———. *Subversives: Antislavery Community in Washington, D.C., 1828–1865*. Baton Rouge: Louisiana State University Press, 2003.

Hedrick, Joan D. *Harriet Beecher Stowe: A Life*. New York: Oxford University Press, 1994.

Hodges, Graham Russell Gao. *David Ruggles: A Radical Black Abolitionist and the Underground Railroad in New York City*. Chapel Hill: University of North Carolina Press, 2010.

Hollyday, Joyce. *On the Heels of Freedom: The American Missionary Association's Bold Campaign to Educate Minds, Open Hearts, and Heal the Soul of a Divided Nation*. New York: Crossroad, 2005.

Holzer, Harold. *Lincoln at Cooper Union: The Speech that Made Abraham Lincoln President*. New York: Simon & Schuster, 2004.

Housley, Donald David. "The Independent: A Study of Religious and Social Opinion, 1848–1870." PhD diss., Pennsylvania State University, 1971.

Howard, John R., ed. *Patriotic Addresses in America and England, from 1850 to 1885, on Slavery, the Civil War, and the Development of Civil Liberty in the United States by Henry Ward Beecher.* Boston, MA: Pilgrim Press, 1887.

———. *Remembrance of Things Past: A Familiar Chronicle of Kinsfolk and Friends Worth While.* New York: Thomas Y. Crowell, 1925.

Howard, Joseph, Jr. *Life of Henry Ward Beecher.* Philadelphia, PA: Hubbard Brothers, 1887.

Isely, W.H. "The Sharps Rifle Episode in Kansas History." *American Historical Review* 12, no. 3 (April 1907): 546–66.

Jackson, Kenneth T., ed. *The Encyclopedia of New York City.* New Haven, CT: Yale University Press, 1995.

Kilde, Jeanne Halgren. *When Church Became Theatre: The Transformation of Evangelical Architecture and Worship in Nineteenth Century America.* New York: Oxford University Press, 2005.

Knox, Thomas W. *Life and Work of Henry Ward Beecher.* Hartford, CT: Hartford, 1887. A facsimile of the first edition, Whitefish, MT: Kessinger, n.d.

Mayer, Henry. *All on Fire: William Lloyd Garrison and the Abolition of Slavery.* New York: St. Martin's Press, 1998.

McPherson, James M. *Battle Cry of Freedom: The Civil War Era.* New York: Oxford University Press, 1988.

———. *Ordeal by Fire: The Civil War and Reconstruction.* 3rd ed. New York: McGraw-Hill, 2001.

———. *The Struggle for Equality: Abolitionists and the Negro in the Civil War and Reconstruction.* Princeton, NJ: Princeton University Press, 1964.

Member of the Church. *Memorial of the Revival in Plymouth Church, During the Early Part of the Year 1858: Comprising Incidents and Narratives, and also Fragments of Sermons, Lectures, etc., by the Pastor.* New York: Clark, Austin & Smith, 1859.

Newby-Alexander, Cassandra L. *An African American History of the Civil War in Hampton Roads.* Charleston, SC: The History Press, 2010.

New York Radical Political Abolitionists. *Proceedings of the Convention of Radical Political Abolitionists, Held at Syracuse, N.Y. on June 26, 27 and 28, 1855.* Facsimile of first edition, Cornell University Library Digital Collections.

New York Union Safety Committee. *Proceedings of the Union Meeting Held at Castle Garden, October 30, 1850.* Facsimile of first edition, Cornell University Library Digital Collections.

Painter, Nell Irvin. *Sojourner Truth: A Life, A Symbol.* New York: W.W. Norton, 1996.

Pantle, Alberta. "The Connecticut Kansas Colony: Letters of Charles B. Lines to the New Haven (Connecticut) Daily Palladium." *Kansas Historical Quarterly* 22 (Spring/Summer 1956): 1–50 and 138–88.

Pauli, Hertha. *Her Name Was Sojourner Truth*. New York: Avon Books, 1962.

Pennington, James W.C. *Fugitive Blacksmith; or, Events in the History of James W.C. Pennington, Pastor of a Presbyterian Church, New York, Formerly a Slave in the State of Maryland, United States*. 2nd ed. London: Charles Gilpin, 1849. Facsimile of first edition, Teddington, UK: Echo Library, 2006.

Potter, David M., and Don E. Fehrenbacher. *The Impending Crisis, 1848–1861*. New York: Harper & Row, 1976.

Quarles, Benjamin. *Black Abolitionists*. New York: Oxford University Press, 1969.

Ray, Florence, and Harriet Charlotte Ray. *Sketch of the Life of Reverend Charles B. Ray*. New York: Press of J.R. Little, 1887.

Reagon, Bernice Johnson, ed. *We'll Understand It Better By and By: Pioneering African American Composers*. Washington, D.C.: Smithsonian Institution Press, 1992.

Reynolds, David S. *Mightier than the Sword: Uncle Tom's Cabin and the Battle for America*. New York: W.W. Norton, 2011.

Richardson, Joe M. *Christian Reconstruction: The American Missionary Association and Southern Blacks, 1861–1890*. Tuscaloosa: University of Alabama Press, 1986.

Ricks, Mary Kay. *Escape on the Pearl: The Heroic Bid for Freedom on the Underground Railroad*. New York: William Morrow, 2007.

Rigler, Ann Marie. "John Zundel as Pedagogue." DMA diss., University of Iowa, 1993.

Ripley, C. Peter, ed. *The Black Abolitionist Papers*. Vol. 2, *Canada*. Chapel Hill: University of North Carolina Press, 1986.

Rose, Willie Lee. *Rehearsal for Reconstruction: The Port Royal Experiment*. New York: Bobbs-Merrill, 1964.

Senior, Nassau William. *American Slavery: A Reprint of an Article on Uncle Tom's Cabin*. London: T. Fellowes, 1856. Facsimile of first edition, collections of the University of Michigan Library.

Sherman, William Tecumseh. *Memoirs*. New York: D. Appleton, 1875. Reprint with a foreword by B.H. Liddell Hart, Bloomington: Indiana University Press, 1957.

Some Memories of John Tasker Howard and His Wife Susan Taylor Raymond. Brooklyn, NY: privately printed, 1909.

Stauffer, John. *The Black Hearts of Men: Radical Abolitionists and the Transformation of Race*. Cambridge, MA: Harvard University Press, 2001.

Stiles, Henry R. *A History of the City of Brooklyn, including the Old Town and Village of Brooklyn, the Town of Bushwick, and the Village and City of Williamsburgh*. 3 vols. Brooklyn, NY: published by subscription, 1869–70.

Still, William. *The Underground Railroad*. Philadelphia, PA: Porter and Coates, 1872. A facsimile of the revised edition published in Hartford in 1886, 2 vols, Teddington, UK: Echo Library, 206.

Stowe, Harriet Beecher. *A Key to Uncle Tom's Cabin; Presenting the Original Facts and Documents Upon Which the Story Is Founded. Together with Corroborative Statements Verifying the Truth of the Work*. Boston, MA: John P. Jewett, 1853. Facsimile of the first edition, Bedford, MA: Applewood, 1998.

———. *Uncle Tom's Cabin; or Life Among the Lowly*. Boston, MA: John P. Jewett, 1852. Reprint, with introductions and annotations by Henry Louis Gates Jr. and Hollis Robbins, eds. *The Annotated Uncle Tom's Cabin*. New York: W.W. Norton, 2007.

Stowe, Lyman Beecher. *Saints, Sinners and Beechers*. New York: Bobbs Merrill Company, 1934. Reprint, Freeport, NY: Books for Libraries Press, 1970.

Swisher, Carl B. *The Taney Period, 1836–64*. Vol. 5, *Oliver Wendell Holmes Devise History of the Supreme Court of the United States*. New York: Macmillan, 1974.

Tappan, Lewis. *The Fugitive Slave Bill: Its History and Constitutionality; With an Account of the Seizure and Enslavement of James Hamlet, and His Subsequent Restoration to Liberty*. New York: William Harned, 1850.

———. *The Life of Arthur Tappan*. New York: Hurd and Houghton, 1871. Reprint, Westport, CT: Negro Universities Press, 1970.

Tevis, Charles V., and Don R. Marquis. *The History of the Fighting Fourteenth: Published in Commemoration of the Muster into the United States Service, May 23, 1861*. Brooklyn, NY: Brooklyn Eagle Press, 1911.

Thompson, Noyes L. *The History of Plymouth Church (Henry Ward Beecher), 1847 to 1872*. New York: G.W. Carleton, 1873.

Tilton, Theodore. "The American Board and American Slavery." Speech at Plymouth Church, Brooklyn, January 28, 1860. New York: William Henry Burr, 1860. Facsimile of first edition, Cornell University Library Digital Collections.

———. "The Negro." Speech at Cooper Institute New York, May 12, 1863. New York: Anti-Slavery Offices, 1863. Facsimile of second edition, Cornell University Library Digital Collections.

U.S. History. Republican Platform, 1856. http://www.ushistory.org/gop/convention_1856republicanplatform.htm.

Von Frank, Albert J. *The Trials of Anthony Burns: Freedom and Slavery in Emerson's Boston*. Cambridge, MA: Harvard University Press, 1998.

Ward, Andrew. *Dark Midnight When I Rise: The Story of the Jubilee Singers Who Introduced the World to the Music of Black America.* New York: Farrar, Straus and Giroux, 2000.

Ward, Samuel Ringgold. *Autobiography of a Fugitive Negro, His Anti-Slavery Labors in the United States, Canada, & England.* London: John Snow, 1855. Reprint, Chicago: Johnson Publishing Company, 1970.

Washington, Margaret. *Sojourner Truth's America.* Urbana: University of Illinois Press, 2009.

Watts, Dale E. "How Bloody Was Bleeding Kansas? Political Killings in Kansas Territory, 1854–1861." *Kansas History: A Journal of the Central Plains* 18, no. 2 (Summer 1995): 116–29.

Webber, Christopher L. *American to the Backbone: The Life of James W.C. Pennington, the Fugitive Slave Who Became One of the First Black Abolitionists.* New York: Pegasus Books, 2011.

Weld, Ralph Foster. *A Tower on the Heights: The Story of the First Presbyterian Church of Brooklyn.* New York: Columbia University Press, 1946.

Wikipedia. "American Missionary Association." http://en.wikipedia.org/wiki/American_Missionary_Association

Wyatt-Brown, Bertram. *Lewis Tappan and the Evangelical War Against Slavery.* Cleveland, OH: Press of Case Western Reserve University, 1969. Reprint, Baton Rouge: Louisiana State University Press, 1997.

PLYMOUTH CHURCH ARCHIVES

Fifield, June [Mrs. Wendell]. Memorandum, dated January 1966, recording her notes in 1945 of a conversation with her husband, Reverend Dr. Wendell Fifield, about his meeting with Branch Rickey.

King, Horatio C. "Henry Ward Beecher's Work for Congregational Singing." Clipping in "Reminiscences," typewritten document in Plymouth Church Archives, donated by King descendant.

King, Martin Luther, Jr. "The American Dream." An Address by Dr. Martin Luther King Jr. on February 10, 1963, at Plymouth Church.

Plymouth Church Annual Reports, 1850–1887, Dismissions, Deaths, Baptisms. Vol. 22.

Plymouth Church Membership: Baptisms, Dismissions, Membership, 1847–1865. Vol. 21.

Plymouth Church Membership Ledger, 1847–1902. Membership arranged alphabetically, initially based on entries in vol. 21 and later membership records.

Plymouth Church Register: Registrar's Book of Membership 1847–1872. Vol. 38.

Plymouth Church Trustees and Annual Meeting Minutes, 1847–1932.

PERSONAL PAPERS

American Missionary Association Papers, Amistad Research Center, New Orleans. Microfilm, Schomburg Center for Research in Black Culture, New York Public Library.

Beecher Family Papers, Yale University Library.

Lewis Tappan Papers, Library of Congress. Microfilm, New York Public Library.

NEWSPAPERS

Brooklyn Daily Eagle.

Brooklyn Star.

Frederick Douglass' Paper.

The Liberator.

National Era.

New York Independent.

New York Journal of Commerce.

New York Times.

New York Tribune.

Radical Abolitionist, vols. 1–4, 1855–58. New York: Negro Universities Press, 1969.

INDEX

ABOUT THE AUTHOR

A longtime member of Plymouth Church, Frank Decker was a member of its governing council from 1993 to 1999. As the council president for three years, he led the church's observance in 1997 of the 150th anniversary of its founding. In this connection, he studied the history of Congregational churches and that of Plymouth—especially in the Civil War era. In 2007, after he retired from the practice of law, he and Lois Rosebrooks prepared and submitted for Plymouth Church an application to the United States National Park Service to have the church listed as a site on the National Underground Railroad Network to Freedom, with the result that the church is so listed.

In 2009, he wrote and presented a paper on Henry Ward Beecher and the Plymouth congregation in the antislavery cause to a symposium on "Congregationalism in the Public Square"; the paper was published in the *International Congregational Journal*. In 2011, he and Lois Rosebrooks submitted a paper on the advocacy of human rights at the church before the Civil War to a conference on New York State history sponsored by the New York Historical Association. He was an associate editor for two volumes of *The Law Practice of Alexander Hamilton* (Columbia University Press, 1964 and 1969), writing commentaries on the documents that were published.

Visit us at
www.historypress.net
....

This title is also available as an e-book